Edith R. Farrell
C. Frederick Farrell, Jr.

SIDE BY SIDE

French & English Grammar

FRENCH GRAMMAR

ENGLISH GRAMMAR

Printed on recyclable paper

PASSPORT BOOKS
a division of *NTC Publishing Group*
Lincolnwood, Illinois USA

ACKNOWLEDGMENTS

We wish to thank our colleagues at the University of Minnesota, Morris: Professors W.D. Spring and Jeffrey L. Burkhart who read the English and French sections, respectively, of the original version of *French & English Grammar Side by Side,* for their patience, humor, and helpful suggestions; Professors Sheryl James and Brigitte Weltlman-Aron (French) and Dorothy Barber, Jeanne Purdy, and James Gremmels (English), who read subsequent editions; and the staff of the UMM Computer Center.

The development of this manual was supported in part by a grant from the Educational Development Program of the University of Minnesota.

DEDICATION

To our students—who had questions

1996 Printing

Published by Passport Books, a division of NTC Publishing Group.
© 1995 by NTC Publishing Group, 4255 West Touhy Avenue,
Lincolnwood (Chicago), Illinois 60646-1975 U.S.A.

Table of Contents / Table des Matières

	Preface	1
	Introduction	3
Chapter One	**Introducing Languages**	**5**
	A Short History of English	*6*
	A Short History of French	*6*
Chapter Two	**Parts of Speech**	**9**
Chapter Three	**Nouns**	**13**
	Subjects and Objects	*18*
	Determiners	*20*
Chapter Four	**Pronouns**	**23**
	Personal Pronouns	*26*
	Possessive Pronouns	*30*
	Reflexive/Reciprocal Pronouns	*32*
	Disjunctive Pronouns	*34*
	Relative Pronouns	*36*
	Demonstrative Pronouns	*40*
	Interrogative Pronouns	*42*
Chapter Five	**Adjectives**	**45**
	Descriptive Adjectives	*48*
	Comparison of Adjectives	*50*
	Proper Adjectives	*52*
	Limiting Adjectives	*52*
	Demonstrative Adjectives	*54*
	Possessive Adjectives	*56*
	Interrogative Adjectives	*56*
	Indefinite Adjectives	*58*
	Other Limiting Adjectives	*58*
	Other Adjectival Forms	*58*
Chapter Six	**Adverbs**	**61**

Chapter Seven **Conjunctions** **67**

Chapter Eight **Interjections** **71**

Chapter Nine **Prepositions** **75**

Chapter Ten **Verbs** **79**

Questions *82*
Verbals *84*
  Infinitives (Present and Past) *84*
  Gerunds *84*
  Participles (Present and Past) *86*
Indicative Mood (Active Voice) *88*
  Present *88*
  Past (Imperfect) *92*
  Future *94*
  Conditional *96*
  Perfect Tenses *98*
    Present Perfect *98*
    Passé Composé *99*
    Past Perfect (Pluperfect) *102*
    Future Perfect *104*
    Conditional Perfect *106*
Passive Voice *108*
Imperative (Command) Mood *110*
Subjunctive Mood (Present Tense) *112*

Appendix I   Pronoun Review 117
Appendix II   Determiners 119
Appendix III Some Common Irregular Verbs 120
Appendix IV   Verbs for Reading 121
Appendix V   Compound Tenses 123
Appendix VI   *Il est... versus C'est...* 124

PREFACE

S ide by Side French & English Grammar presents the essential elements of French grammar—usually covered in a high school program or in the first year of college French—"side by side" with their English counterparts. This comparative/contrastive approach allows students to build on what they already know, as they see the ways in which English and French are similar, and to avoid potential trouble spots.

Side by Side French & English Grammar has been used in both high school and university French classes and even in some English classes for a few students who were having trouble in understanding their English grammar text. Its vocabulary is, for the most part, limited to the 1500 most frequently used French words.

It has been used as:

1. a reference book for beginning students, for whom the standard works are too complex to be useful. This allows them a means for independent inquiry.

2. a means of quick review of material forgotten over the summer or material missed because of illness.

3. a means of helping a student in a new school to catch up with the class.

4. a means of organizing or summarizing material presented in the primary text, especially for students whose learning style favors an "organized approach."

5. a means of providing a common background for talking about language with students who have studied English in different ways so that their study of French will show them something of how language works, one of the expectations of many college language requirements.

6. a source of an alternate way of explaining grammatical points in both English and French to relieve the classroom teacher of the task.

Special features of the book that you and your students may find useful include:

1. a standard format in each section that introduces the part of speech and answers the most common questions about it.

2. Quick Check Charts (marked by a ✔) that allow students to express themselves with more confidence since they can independently check their sentences against a model.

3. appendices that identify and summarize trouble spots such as the differences between the forms of the relative and interrogative pronouns, or items for passive learning only, such as the verb tenses needed specifically for formal reading.

We hope that this text will provide ways for you and your students to increase independent work and to adapt material to different learning styles and situations.

EDITH R. FARRELL & C. FREDERICK FARRELL, JR.
The University of Minnesota, Morris

INTRODUCTION

TO THE STUDENT

This manual grew out of a series of supplements to a French grammar text. Its purpose is to help you learn French more easily.

Many students have had trouble with foreign languages because they have not looked carefully enough, or critically enough, at their own. Struggles with your own language took place at such an early age that you have forgotten the times when it seemed difficult. Now it seems perfectly natural to you, and it is hard to adapt to different ways of expressing ideas.

Everything in this book has been classified and arranged to show you English and your new language "side by side." You may be surprised at how many things are done the same way.

Information that is the same for both English and French is usually *not* repeated on facing pages. If you find a section is omitted under the French, look to your left and find it in English. The English meaning of a French example is usually on the left-hand page, too.

WHY GRAMMAR?

People can speak, read, or write their native language, at least to a reasonable degree, without studying formal grammar (the rules governing how we say, change, and arrange words to express our ideas).

Just by being around others we hear millions of examples, and the patterns we hear become a part of us. Even babies start with correct basic patterns (subject-verb-object) even though words may be missing or incorrect: "Me wants cookie!"

Knowledge of grammar helps a great deal, though, in testing new and more complex words or patterns or in analyzing your writing to discover where a sentence went wrong or how it could be more effective. Sometimes "It sounds right (or wrong)" won't help.

All of the explanations given in this book are of *standard* English or French. Sometimes you may think, "I don't say that!" The important word here is "say." We often ignore some rules in conversation, or even in informal writing such as friendly letters. At other times, though, if you are writing an important paper or giving a speech, you may want to use the standard form in order to make the best possible impression. You will also find that knowing grammar will help you in your study of language.

In learning a foreign language, grammar is necessary because it tells you how to choose the right word—or the right form of a word that you are using for the first time. It is not the way that you acquired your native language as a child, but it is an efficient way for adults who want to express more complex ideas and do not want to make any more mistakes than absolutely necessary.

Grammar saves you time and many mistakes by guiding you in your choices.

CHAPTER ONE

INTRODUCING

LANGUAGES

A Short History of English

What we now know as England was settled in the fifth and sixth centuries A.D. by Germanic tribes like the Angles, Saxons, and Jutes, all speaking their own, but similar, dialects. Later, in the ninth century, Scandinavian invaders came, bringing their languages, which also contributed to English. Political power determined the centers of learning, which contained the writings in Latin of continental literature as well as the contributions made by the inhabitants of Great Britain. By the ninth century, the primary center was in Wessex, due to the Viking invasions in the north, and so the West Saxon dialect became standard as Old English. It was heavily inflected with endings on nouns to show many cases and on verbs to show time and person.

This was the language current in 1066, when William the Conqueror, from the province of Normandy in what is now France, won the battle of Hastings and became ruler of England. The natives knew no French; William and his followers did not speak Old English. For a long time each group continued to speak its own language; but gradually they merged. Since the governing group spoke French, we often find that words for work, home, or plainer things come from Old English, while words for leisure or art products come from French.

Wamba, the jester in Sir Walter Scott's *Ivanhoe,* made a joke of this, saying that cows and pigs were Anglo-Saxon while the peasants took care of them, but became French (beef, pork) when they were ready to be eaten. In the same way, *house* looks and sounds like the German word *Haus,* but *mansion* comes from the French, *maison.*

If you are looking for a cognate (a word that looks like and means the same thing as a word in French) to help you remember a meaning, try to think of a more "distinguished" word:

donner → to give (think of "donate")   *signifier* → to mean (think of "signify")

Latin, which remained the language of the church, and therefore of learning in general, also influenced English. Around 1500, about 25% of the known Latin vocabulary was added to English. English, therefore, is basically a Germanic language, but one to which large portions of French and Latin were added.

Since the French also borrowed from Latin in the Renaissance, we have many words in common, but they are not the everyday words. Compare the following:

Germanic root (Common)	**French root** (Elegant)	**Latin root** (Learned)
ask	question	interrogate
goodness	virtue	probity
better	improve	ameliorate
rider	cavalier	equestrian

Knowing basic French words may help you recognize the meaning of new English words that you see.

A Short History of French

French is one of the Romance languages, like Spanish, Italian, and others, that have grown out of Latin. When Julius Caesar invaded Gaul (now France) in the first century B.C., he found different people with different languages. When they tried to learn Latin from the Roman soldiers—who were not language teachers—they learned "mistakes," and they also pronounced the words a little differently because they continued to use sounds that were familiar in their own language. They had a foreign accent. Other peoples, like those in northern Italy and Spain, did the same thing.

This continued until the "Latin" of different countries had evolved into different, even though related, languages. Now, while you can guess at words and even forms and rules in a different Romance language, based on your knowledge of one, a speaker of Spanish cannot be understood by a speaker of French or vice versa. As in English, Latin words were added

A Short History of French (continued)

to French in the sixteenth century to form a "learned" language. These words are generally used only by educated people and so have not changed over the years as have the ones with a 2000-year history.

Many French people feel much more strongly about their language than we do about English and are very careful about how they use it. They also have the *Académie française,* which determines the standard language. Since they are concerned about what is right and what isn't, French changes more slowly than English. However, all languages change, and the trend is to inflect them less and less. Distinctions that seem to be too hard or unnecessary die out.

Different languages chose different things to drop. For example, in Latin, and other older languages, every noun had gender, number, and case (which told you its function, that is, how it was used in the sentence). German still has all three as very important elements.

In English, we pay little attention to grammatical gender, but nouns still have number (singular and plural) and one extra case (the possessive), while pronouns have an objective case also. The other cases are expressed by word order and prepositions. French has no cases for nouns anymore, but does keep grammatical gender as well as number. You will notice other instances in which French and English emphasize different things. Comparing languages is interesting because it shows us what different people think is important. Let's look at a noun in Germanic languages:

	Modern German		**Old English**		**Modern English**
subj.	der König	die Könige	se cyning	tha cyningas	the king(s)
gen.	des Königs	der Könige	thoes cyning	thara cyninga	the king's(s')
dat.	dem König	den Königen	thaem cyninge	thaem cyningum	to the king(s)
obj.	den König	die Könige	thone cyning	tha cyningas	the king(s)

The declension (giving all the cases of a noun) is further complicated by having feminine and neuter nouns whose definite articles and endings are different from this masculine example, and irregular nouns, which have different rules. Adjectives also have different endings for each gender and each case. For a verb sample, let's compare Latin and French with English:

Latin		**Modern French**		**English**	
habeo	habemus	j'ai	nous avons	I have	we have
habes	habetis	tu as	vous avez	you have	you have
habet	habent	il a	ils ont	he has	they have

You will notice that there are some differences. The endings in Latin are so distinctive that it is not necessary to mention the subject. This is still true in languages like Spanish and Italian. The "h" is often not pronounced in many European languages and never in standard French. "V" and "b" are very similar sounds, and they change places easily. In Spanish they are almost identical. Modern English is the least inflected of the five languages shown here, French is next, and then the others.

**CHAPTER
TWO**

PARTS OF SPEECH

INTRODUCING THE PARTS OF SPEECH

Both English and French words are classified by "parts of speech." You may have learned these in elementary school without really seeing any use for them. They are important because different rules apply to the different categories. In your own language, you do this naturally, unless the word is new to you. You know to say "one horse, two horses," adding an "s" to make it plural. You do not try to apply a noun's rule to verbs and say "I am, we ams." Instead, you say "we are." Using the wrong set of rules sometimes happens to people in a foreign language, though, because all of the forms are new, so nothing "sounds wrong." To avoid this kind of mistake, pay attention to the part of speech when you learn a new vocabulary word.

Parts of speech help you to identify words so that even if a word is used in several ways (and this happens in both English and French) you can find the French equivalent. For instance, "that" can be:

1. a conjunction:

   I know **that** Mary is coming. → *Je sais* **que** *Marie vient.*

2. a demonstrative adjective:

   That person is impossible. → **Cette** *personne est impossible.*

3. a pronoun:

   I didn't know **that.** → *Je ne savais pas* **cela.**

When you know the parts of speech, the fact that a word is used several ways in English won't cause you to choose the wrong one in French.

Here is a list of the parts of speech. The terms are defined by a traditional description, by the form that identifies them, and by their function (as the more modern structural linguists think of them).

NOUNS

1. Names or words standing for persons, places, things, abstracts:

   John, man, Paris, city, table, justice

2. Words that usually become plural by adding "-s" (or in a few other ways):

   book, books; fox, foxes; child, children

3. Words that serve as subjects, objects, or complements:

   John *is here. She read the* **book.** *There is* **Mary.**

PRONOUNS

1. Words that substitute for nouns:

   John is already here. Have you seen **him** *(John)?*

2. Words that are used when no noun is available:

   It *is raining.* **They** *say…* **You** *never know.*

3. Words that serve the same function as nouns:

   He *is here.* **He** *loves* **her.** *There* **it** *is.*

ADJECTIVES

1. Words that modify, limit, or qualify a noun or pronoun:

   big, red, specious, happy

2. Words that may be inflected (change form) to make comparisons:

   large, larger, largest; serious, more serious, most serious

VERBS

1. Words that express action or existence:

   speak, learn, run, be, have, feel

2. Words that can be inflected to show person (*I **am,** he **is***), time (*I **sing,** I **sang***), voice (*I **write,** it **is written***), and mood (*if I **am** here, if I **were** you*).

ADVERBS

1. Words that modify verbs, adjectives, or other adverbs by telling how, when, where, or how much:

   *We'll come **soon.** It's **really** big. They do it **very** well.*

2. Words that can show comparison between verbs (as adjectives do for nouns):

   rapidly, more rapidly, most rapidly; soon, sooner, soonest

PREPOSITIONS

1. Words that express place, time, etc., and show the relationship between two parts of a sentence:

   in, on, of

2. Words that are not inflected (words that never change form).

3. Words that have a noun or pronoun as their object:

   ***on** it, **in** a minute, **of** a sort*

   These groups are called **prepositional phrases.**

CONJUNCTIONS

1. Coordinating conjunctions (*and, but, so,* etc.) connect words, phrases, or clauses that are grammatically equal:

   *John **and** Mary*

2. Subordinating conjunctions (*because, if, when,* etc.) connect subordinate clauses to the main clause:

   ***When** you see it, you will believe me.*

INTERJECTIONS

1. Exclamations.

2. Words that can be used alone or in sentences:

   ***Darn! Oh,** Mary, is it true?*

NOUNS

Introducing Nouns in English

WHAT ARE THEY? See the definitions on p. 10.

WHAT FORMS DO THEY HAVE?

NOTE: Nouns are often preceded by **determiners** (see p. 20):

a book, *the* book, *my* book, *two* books, etc.

Nouns are considered to have **gender, number,** and **case.**

Gender: We use masculine or feminine gender only for something that is male or female:

man, woman, tigress

All other nouns are neuter. Gender makes no difference in English except when there are two forms for one noun (e.g., *actor, actress*) or when the nouns are replaced by pronouns (e.g., *he, she, it*).

Number: Most nouns have different forms for the singular and the plural and add "-s" or "-es." Some have irregular plurals:

mouse, mice; man, men; child, children

Case: There is only one extra case in English, the possessive or genitive. It is formed by adding "-'s" to the singular or "-s'" to plurals ending in "-s":

Mary's book, the *book's* pages, the *books'* pages

NOTE: We can also ignore the possessive case and use "of," although this form is less common when a person is involved:

the theories *of Kant,* the pages *of the book*

WHAT USES DO THEY HAVE? The three most common uses of nouns are as subjects, objects, or complements (see p. 18):

Mrs. Dupont is French. (as a subject)
Mrs. Dupont, a French woman, is visiting us. (as an appositive)
He has a pencil. (as a direct object of the verb)
She gave the hat to John. (as an indirect object of the verb)
We are in the room. (as an object of the preposition, *in*)
It is a valuable book. (as a complement)
I have my history text. (as an adjective)

(Continued on p. 16)

Introducing Nouns in French

WHAT ARE THEY? See the definitions on p. 10.

WHAT FORMS DO THEY HAVE?

NOTE: Nouns are often preceded by **determiners** (see p. 21):
un livre, *le* livre, *mon* livre, *deux* livres, etc.

Nouns are considered to have **gender** and **number** but not **case.**

Gender: All nouns in French are either masculine or feminine. There is no neuter. When you learn a noun, you also learn whether it is masculine or feminine.

The gender of nouns is very important in French, since their determiners and the adjectives accompanying them must be in the same gender. If a word is preceded by *le* or *un*, it is masculine; *la* and *une* designate a feminine word. *L'* is placed before any word beginning with a vowel or a mute (silent) "h" to make it easier to say. *L'* does not tell you which gender the word is.

Number: Most French nouns add "-s" to form the plural, but they also need a plural article, because the final "-s" is not pronounced. *Les* replaces both *le* and *la* and is used for both masculine and feminine. *Des* is plural for *un* and *une.*

There are some common irregular plurals. For example, words ending in "-al" usually change to "-aux" and those ending in "-eau" and "-eu" change to "-eaux" and "-eux":

le journal, les journaux; l'eau, les eaux; le lieu, les lieux

Words ending in "-s," "-x," or "-z" do not change in the plural:

un cours, des cours; le nez, les nez

Proper nouns never change:

les Duval

Case: Nouns never change for case in French. Possession is formed with the preposition *de* plus an article if one is needed:

*les théories **de Kant,** les pages **du livre***

WHAT USES DO THEY HAVE? Nouns are used in the same way in French as in English. Compare these sentences with the examples opposite:

***Madame Dupont** est française.*
*Mme Dupont, une **Française,** nous rend visite.*
*Il a un **crayon.***
*Elle a donné le chapeau à **Jean.***
*Nous sommes dans la **pièce.***
*C'est un **livre** précieux.*
*J'ai mon texte **d'histoire.*** (Rarely is a noun used alone as an adjective in French; a phrase, usually with *de*, is used.)

(Continued on p. 17)

WHAT KINDS ARE THERE? There are a number of different classifications of nouns. Here are two important ones:

1. **Common** and **proper**

   Common nouns are the words applied to a class of individuals. They begin with a lower-case letter:

   student, country, cat, language

   Proper nouns name a specific individual within a class. They begin with a capital letter:

   Miss Jones, France, Kitty, English

2. **Countable** and **mass**

   Countable nouns are ones that can be counted:

   one pencil, two pencils, etc.

   Mass nouns cannot be separated into individuals; they cannot be counted:

   salt, weather

Introducing Nouns
in French
(continued)

WHAT KINDS ARE THERE?

1. **Common** and **proper**

For the most part, French is the same as English, but there are a few important differences. Nouns for languages, days of the week, and months are common nouns. They do not require a capital letter:

     English → *l'anglais*   Monday → *lundi*   October → *octobre*

2. **Countable** and **mass**

These nouns follow the same principle in French as in English. Using them, however, frequently requires a **partitive** construction in French (see p. 22).

INTRODUCING SUBJECTS AND OBJECTS

A. SUBJECTS

Subjects are most frequently nouns or pronouns. The subject of a verb is the person or thing that *is* or *is doing* something:

> **Mary** and **I** are here. **John** speaks French. Are **they** (the texts) arriving today?

✔ QUICK CHECK

☐ Ask yourself: *Who* is here? *Who* speaks French? *What* is arriving?

The answer is the **subject.**

In normal word order, the subject comes before the verb. The subject is often, but not always, the first word in the sentence or clause.

B. SUBJECT COMPLEMENTS

These are words or phrases that define or complete our idea about the subject:

> Mr. White is a **professor.** Jeanne and Alice are **Americans.**

C. DIRECT OBJECTS

Some systems of grammar call these **object complements.** The name matters less than the ability to recognize their important function. Direct objects are usually nouns or pronouns that directly receive the verb's action. In normal word order the direct object comes after the verb:

> Mary hates **John.** She hates **him.**
> The professor is giving a **test.** He is giving **it.**

✔ QUICK CHECK

☐ Ask yourself: Who *is hated?* What *is being given?*

The answer is the **direct object.**

D. INDIRECT OBJECTS

These objects tell us who or what is indirectly affected by the verb's action. It answers the question to whom or for whom something is done:

> Speak **to me!**

COMBINATIONS

Some verbs (e.g., *give, tell, buy*) can have more than one object. Besides the direct object, there can also be an indirect object. With the subject, this can give you three nouns or pronouns with different functions even in a short sentence:

> **Robert** gives **the book to Alice.**
> (S.)   (D.O.)   (I.O.)

> **Robert** gives **Alice the book.**
> (S.)   (I.O.)   (D.O.)

> **He** gives **it to her.**
> (S.)   (D.O.) (I.O.)

Notice that the two possible word orders do not have any effect on which object is direct and which is indirect. The word order in English does determine whether or not we use the word *to.*

✔ **QUICK CHECK**

☐ To analyze the sample sentences, ask:

Who gives? Answer: *Robert* or *he* → **subject**

Who or what is given? Answer: the *book* or *it* → **direct object**

To whom/for whom/to what/for what is it given? Answer: *Alice* or *her* → **indirect object**

E. OBJECTS OF PREPOSITIONS

We have learned that all prepositions must have objects (p. 11). These objects come immediately after the preposition:

*on the **table**, on **it**; after **Peter**, after **him***

NOTE: In questions and relative clauses (p. 76), this rule is often ignored in English, and we use the preposition alone at the end of the sentence:

***Who** did you give it **to**?* INSTEAD OF ***To whom** did you give it?*

The second is standard English. French uses the same patterns as standard English.

PROBLEMS WITH DIRECT AND INDIRECT OBJECTS

English and French verbs meaning the same thing usually take the same kind of object, but not always. They must be learned as vocabulary items.

Direct Object in English

*He **obeys** his parents.*
*He **phones** Ann.*
*I **am answering** the letter.*
*Mary always **asks** John.*

Object of a Preposition in English

*They **look at** the television.*
*Monica **is looking for** the book.*
*Michael **is waiting for** the teacher.*
*The student **listens to** the teacher.*

Indirect Object in French

*Il **obéit à** ses parents.*
*Il **téléphone à** Anne.*
*Je **réponds à** la lettre.*
*Marie **demande** toujours **à** Jean.*

Direct Object in French

*Ils **regardent** la télévision.*
*Monique **cherche** le livre.*
*Michel **attend** le professeur.*
*L'étudiant **écoute** le professeur.*

Introducing Determiners in English

WHAT ARE THEY? Determiners are words that introduce nouns and their adjectives. They usually come first in a noun phrase:

the red book, *a* tall boy, *each* window, *several* students

WHAT KINDS ARE THERE? Many kinds of words can serve as determiners: definite articles, indefinite articles, partitives, numbers, general words like *each, either, several,* etc. Some types of adjectives (possessives, demonstratives, interrogatives) can also be determiners. They are discussed in the adjective section.

WHAT FORMS DO THEY HAVE? The **definite article** is always written *the,* but it is pronounced like *thee* before a vowel and some "h's" (e.g., *the book* and *the apple* or *the hour*). The **indefinite article** is *a, an* in the singular; *some* in the plural. *An* is used before words beginning with a vowel or silent "h." Other forms of determiners do not change their spelling or pronunciation.

WHAT USES DO THEY HAVE?

Definite Articles. *The* indicates a specific noun:

The book (the one you wanted) is on the table.

Indefinite Articles. *A, an* refers to any one of a class:

I see *a* boy (not a specific one).

Others. Their use is determined by what you mean:
some boys, *few* boys, *several* boys, *ten* boys

Introducing Determiners in French

WHAT FORMS DO THEY HAVE?

Definite Articles. The form of the definite article depends on the gender and number of the noun and on whether it begins with a vowel or, often, an "h." Words beginning with an "h" that take the same determiner as a consonant are marked with an * or some other sign in your vocabulary list or dictionary (e.g., *le *héros*):

Gender/Number	Before a Consonant	Before a Vowel and Many "h's"
Masculine singular	*le jour*	*l'homme* (but *le héros*)
Feminine singular	*la télévision*	*l'étudiante*
Plural	*les jours*	*les hommes* (links as a "z" sound)
	les télévisions	*les étudiantes*

NOTE: These forms can also be combined with the prepositions *à* and *de* (see p. 77).

Indefinite Articles. Indefinite articles agree with the noun, just as the definite articles do. However, because they have a consonant at the end, they do not change spelling before a vowel. Instead, in speaking, we link the "n" or "s" sound and pronounce it at the beginning of the next word (e.g., *un ami*):

Gender/Number	Before a Consonant	Before a Vowel and Many "h's"
Masculine singular	*un jour*	*un ami* (links as an "n" sound)
Feminine singular	*une télévision*	*une amie*
Plural	*des jours*	*des amis* (links as a "z" sound)
	des télévisions	*des amies*

Partitives. These are normally formed by the preposition *de* plus the appropriate definite article:

du pain, *de la* glace, *de l'eau*, *des* livres

NOTE: There are four situations where *de* is used alone:

1. normally after an expression of quantity:

   beaucoup de vin; *tant de* gens

   Exceptions: *bien des* gens, *la plupart des* étudiants; when referring to specific nouns:

   beaucoup des étudiants de cette classe → many of the students in this class

2. after a negative:

   Il *n'y a pas d'argent* dans mon sac.

3. after an expression including *de:*

   J'ai besoin d'amis.

4. before a plural adjective:

   Jean et Jeanne sont *de bons* enfants.

(Continued on p. 22)

Others. Each must be learned separately as a vocabulary word. Some determiners change spelling for gender or number. Check this as you learn new words such as:

plusieurs; chaque; tout, toute, tous, toutes

WHAT USES DO THEY HAVE?

Definite articles are used:

1. before a specific noun as in English.

2. before a noun used in a general sense:

*Je déteste **la** télévision.* → I hate television (generally speaking).

***La** guerre est mauvaise.* → War (in general) is bad.

3. before many kinds of nouns that take no article in English:

languages → *l'anglais*   qualities → ***la** beauté*   countries → ***la** France*

titles → ***le** général*   qualified proper names → ***le** vieux Paris*

Indefinite articles are used:

1. for the number "one":

***un** étudiant, **une** étudiante*

2. for any member of a group or category:

*Paul a **un** bon professeur.*

Partitives are used to express part of a whole. There is no English equivalent for this construction. In English we often don't make this distinction and put nothing before the noun:

***L'argent** est utile.* → Money (in general) is useful.

*J'ai **de l'argent**.* → I have (some) money.

Since we just say "money" in both cases, we have to stop and think. Do we mean *all* money, money *in general* (which takes the definite article), OR are we speaking of just *some* money (what we have today, for example), in which case we must use the partitive. Let's look at some examples:

1. I like ice cream. (All) ice cream is good. → *J'aime **la** glace. **La** glace est bonne.*

But, much as I like it, I can consume only a *part* of this whole quantity, so:

I'd like ice cream, please. → *Je voudrais **de la** glace, s'il vous plaît.*

2. Students at the university (all of them) are intelligent. → ***Les** étudiants à l'université sont intelligents.*

But not all of them will fit into this classroom, so:

There are students in the classroom. → *Il y a **des** étudiants dans la salle de classe.*

Others. Most of these are used as they are in English. See also Appendix II (p. 119).

CHAPTER FOUR

PRONOUNS

Introducing Pronouns in English

WHAT ARE THEY? See the definitions on p. 10.

WHAT FORMS DO THEY HAVE? Like nouns, pronouns have **gender, number,** and **case,** but more distinctions are made. They also change depending on the **person.**

Person. We distinguish three persons. The first person is the one who is speaking (*I, me, we, us*). The second person is the one being spoken to (*you*). The third person is the one being spoken about (*he, she, it, they, them*). Both pronouns and verbs will be listed by these persons.

Gender. Some, but not all, pronouns can be distinguished by gender. *I* can refer to either a man or a woman. *She,* however, is always feminine, *he* always masculine, and *it,* even if it refers to an animal, is always neuter.

Number. Each of the three persons may be either singular or plural.

Case. Pronouns show more cases than nouns: the subjective, possessive, and objective (*I, mine, me; she, hers, her*). These are discussed under USES below.

WHAT USES DO THEY HAVE? Personal pronouns have the same functions as nouns. They may be:

1. subjects → *She* is here.
2. direct objects → I like *them.*
3. indirect objects → I am giving *him* the book.
4. objects of a preposition → The question is hard for *me.*
5. complements → It is *she* who is speaking.

WHAT KINDS ARE THERE? There are several different kinds of pronouns, each discussed individually:

1. **personal** (see p. 26)
2. **possessive** (see p. 30)
3. **reflexive/reciprocal** (see p. 32)
4. **disjunctive** (see p. 34)
5. **relative** (see p. 36)
6. **demonstrative** (see p. 40)
7. **interrogative** (see p. 42)

Introducing Pronouns in French

Definitions, forms, and uses are the same in French as in English. However, there are three other important things to know.

1. In French, the personal pronoun for "you" has two forms in the singular—the familiar (*tu*) and the formal (*vous*). The plural form is always *vous*.

   Tu is used for:

members of the family	animals
close friends	inferiors (it can be an insult)
fellow students (or colleagues)	yourself
children (under about 13)	God

   Vous is used for everyone else. Be careful about this. Unless the case is clear (a dog, a small child), use *vous* and allow the French person to suggest using *tu*. A complication is that this use is largely personal preference. Some people never use *tu* except for family, children, and animals.

2. **On** (the equivalent of the English pronoun "one") is listed with the personal pronouns because it is used very frequently in French—much more so than "one" in American English, which tends to use "you" or "they" for indefinite subjects (e.g., "It's true, you know," or "They say that...").

   On may replace any pronoun to avoid being too personal. You should understand from the circumstances who it is:

   On est fâché. → One is angry.

   On est invité à... is more modest than "We got an invitation to..."

   However, regardless of the pronoun replaced, *on* always takes a third person singular verb.

3. Remember that there is no neuter in French: *il* replaces masculine things as well as people, and *elle,* the feminine ones. In the third person plural, *ils* is used both for groups of masculine people (or things) and for mixed groups. *Elles* is used only for all feminine groups.

Personal Pronouns in English

PERSONAL PRONOUNS IN ENGLISH

A. SUBJECT PRONOUNS (Subjects of verbs; see p. 18.)

Person	Singular	Plural
1	I	we
2	you	you
3	he, she, it, one (indefinite)	they

John gives a present. → ***He*** *gives it.* (third person singular)
Mary and I arrive. → ***We*** *arrive.* (first person plural)

B. DIRECT OBJECT PRONOUNS (See p. 18.)

Person	Singular	Plural
1	me	us
2	you	you
3	him, her, it, one	them

*He sees **me**, and I see **you**. You found **them**.*

(Continued on p. 28)

Personal Pronouns in French

A. SUBJECT PRONOUNS (Subjects of verbs; see p. 18.)

A subject pronoun must always be the same gender and number as the noun that it replaces.

Person	Singular	Plural
1	je (note small "j")	nous
2	tu	vous
3	il, elle, on	ils, elles

B. DIRECT OBJECT PRONOUNS (See p. 18.)

Person	Singular	Plural
1	me	nous
2	te	vous
3	le (masc.) la (fem.)	les (masc. and fem.)

*Il **me** voit, et je **vous** vois. Vous **les** avez trouvés.*

NOTE: The final letter of a singular form elides (is dropped) before a vowel or mute "h":

*Il **m'**aime. Elle **l'**adore.*

For the third person, choosing the correct pronoun is easy if you remember that the pronoun is the same as the definite article:

*Je cherche **le** livre.* (Definite article and pronoun are **le**.) → *Je **le** cherche.*

Position. Except in affirmative commands, an object pronoun in French is placed directly before the conjugated verb or infinitive of which it is the object:

*Il **me** voit. Je **vous** vois.* → He sees me. I see you.
*Je cherche le livre. Je **le** cherche.* → I am looking for it.
*Pierre aime lire les lettres. Pierre aime **les** lire.* → Peter likes to read them.

In a question or a negative sentence, the pronoun stays in this same position with respect to the verb, i.e., directly BEFORE it.

*Avez-vous les billets? **Les** avez-vous?* → Do you have them?
*Je n'ai pas les billets. Je ne **les** ai pas.* → I don't have them.
*N'a-t-il pas les billets? Ne **les** a-t-il pas?* → Doesn't he have them?

The only exception is affirmative commands. In negative commands, the pronoun stays before the verb. (For additional comments on pronouns with commands, see p. 111.)

*Donnez le pain à Marie. Donnez-**le** à Marie.* → Give it to Mary.
*Ne **le** donnez pas à Marie.* → Don't give it to Mary.

(Continued on p. 29)

*Personal
Pronouns
in English
(continued)*

C. INDIRECT OBJECT PRONOUNS (See p. 18.)

Person	Singular	Plural
1	(to, for) me	(to, for) us
2	(to, for) you	(to, for) you
3	(to, for) him, her, it, one	(to, for) them

*He writes **her** a letter. They send the letter **to us.**
I bought a dress **for her.** I got a ticket **for them.***

D. OBJECTS OF PREPOSITIONS

After a preposition, we use the same form of the pronoun as for direct objects.

NOTE: Beware of compound pronoun subjects or objects. They remain in the same case that would have been used for a single subject or object:

I am French. **She** and **I** are French.
This is between **us.** This is between **you** and **me.**

E. WORD ORDER

When there are two pronoun objects in English, the direct object comes before the indirect:

*He shows **it** to **them.***

When a noun and a pronoun are used together, word order can vary:

He shows the **book** to **them.**
        (D.O.)   (I.O.)

He shows **them** the **book.**
        (I.O.)   (D.O.)

Personal Pronouns in French (continued)

C. INDIRECT OBJECT PRONOUNS (See p. 18.)

The indirect object is used more frequently in French where we would use a preposition plus object in English.

Person	Singular	Plural
1	me	nous
2	te	vous
3	lui	leur
	(masc. and fem.)	(masc. and fem.)

These pronouns are in the same position in the sentence as the direct object pronouns:

*Je **lui** ai acheté une robe.* → I bought her a dress; I bought a dress for her.
*Je **leur** ai procuré un billet.* → I got them a ticket; I got a ticket for them.

D. OBJECTS OF PREPOSITIONS

Most prepositions require the disjunctive pronouns in French (see p. 35). However, there are two pronouns that replace both a preposition and its object:

En replaces **de** plus *a noun:*

*Il a besoin **d'argent**. Il **en** a besoin.* → He needs some.
***En** a-t-elle?* → Does she have some (any)?

Y replaces **à** plus *a noun* or any *place preposition* plus *a noun:*

*Je pense souvent **à mon lycée**. J'**y** pense souvent.* → I often think about it.
*Le billet est **dans mon sac**. Le billet **y** est.* → The ticket is there.

E. WORD ORDER

Some verbs often have more than one pronoun object:

*Il **le leur** montre.* → He shows it to them.

To determine the order of pronouns before the verb:

1. Remember "1-2-3." First person pronoun comes before second, second before third.
2. If there are *two third person objects,* put the *direct object before the indirect. Y* and *en* always come last, and in that order.

✔ **QUICK CHECK** (normal French word order)

SUBJECT	+	me	+	le	+	lui	+	y	+	en	+	VERB
		te		la		leur						
		nous		les								
		vous										

NOTE: Remember that *me, te, le, la* will become *m', t',* and *l'* before a vowel or mute "h."

(Continued on p. 30)

*Personal
Pronouns
in French
(continued)*

In affirmative commands, the objects *follow* the verb. Put the *direct object before the indirect* regardless of person:

*Donnez-**le-moi**!* → Give it to me!
*Montrez-**les-lui**!* → Show them to him (her)!

✔ **QUICK CHECK** (for affirmative commands only)

		D.O.		I.O.				
VERB	+	le (l') la (l') les	+	moi (m') toi (t') nous vous lui leur	+	y	+	en

NOTE: *Moi, toi, le, la* become *m', t,* and *l'* before a vowel or mute "h."

Possessive Pronouns in English

WHAT ARE THEY? A possessive pronoun replaces a possessive adjective (or a noun in the possessive) and a noun:

*It's **my book**.* → *It's **mine**.*   *It's **Anne's car**.* → *It's **hers**.*

WHAT FORMS DO THEY HAVE? They have person and number. In the third person singular, they also have gender. They do not have case; that is, they have the same form no matter what function they fulfill in the sentence:

Person	Singular	Plural
1	mine	ours
2	yours	yours
3	his, hers, its, one's	theirs

As long as you know the person, gender, and number of the one who is the possessor, (e.g., Mary), there is only one choice for the pronoun—*hers*:

*You have your book; where is **Mary's** book (**her** book)?*

To avoid repeating "book," we replace it and the possessive noun or adjective in front of it. "Mary's" (or "her") is third person, feminine, singular. Therefore *hers* is the proper pronoun:

*You have your book; where is **hers**?*

Possessive Pronouns in French

WHAT FORMS ARE THERE? In French, possessive pronouns have person and number as in English, but they also have gender changes for all singular forms. Person is a vocabulary problem and corresponds to the *person who owns*. Gender and number are determined by *what is owned*:

le livre de Marie	Mary's book	*les chemises de Jean*	John's shirts
son livre	her book	*ses chemises*	his shirts
le sien	hers	*les siennes*	his

Even though Mary is female, since "book" is masculine, it requires that the pronoun be masculine singular (*son livre, le sien*). Likewise, although John is male, "shirts" is feminine and plural. Therefore, it requires a feminine plural pronoun (*ses chemises, les siennes*).

Person	Singular	Plural
1	le mien, la mienne, les miens, les miennes	le nôtre, la nôtre, les nôtres
2	le tien, la tienne, les tiens, les tiennes	le vôtre, la vôtre, les vôtres
3	le sien, la sienne, les siens, les siennes (his, hers, its)	le leur, la leur, les leurs (theirs)

Reflexive/Reciprocal Pronouns in English

WHAT ARE THEY? The reflexive pronouns are defined as pronoun objects or complements that refer to the same person(s) or thing(s) as another element in the sentence, most frequently the subject.

WHAT FORMS DO THEY HAVE?

Person	Singular	Plural	Reciprocal
1	myself	ourselves	each other or one another
2	yourself	yourselves	each other or one another
3	himself, herself, itself, oneself	themselves	each other or one another

WHAT USES DO THEY HAVE? Reflexive pronouns are used as objects of a verb or a preposition.

WHAT KINDS ARE THERE? Reflexive pronouns are usually used only when the subjects act directly on themselves or do something for themselves directly:

Paul cut *himself. I* told *myself* it didn't matter.

Occasionally, they are used idiomatically:

They always enjoy *themselves.*

For a mutual or reciprocal action, we use *each other* or *one another*. This expression does not change form:

They congratulated *each other. We* talked to *each other* yesterday. *You* two saw *each other* last night.

NOTE: In English we often omit reflexive and reciprocal objects and expect everyone to understand what we mean:

We **talked** *yesterday.* ("to each other" is understood)

Or we shift to a construction that requires no object:

Paul **got hurt.** ("hurt himself" is understood)

However, consider the sentence:

We washed this morning.

It is meaningless if you have not heard the rest of the conversation. It may mean:

We washed ourselves (got washed). *OR*
We washed our clothes (did the laundry).

Reflexive/Reciprocal Pronouns in French

WHAT FORMS DO THEY HAVE? They are the same as the direct and indirect object pronouns, except for the third person, and come in the same position in the sentence.

Person	Singular	Plural
1	me (m')	nous
2	te (t')	vous
3	se (s')	se (s')

WHAT USES DO THEY HAVE? These pronouns are used as objects (either direct or indirect) of the verb (see p. 18). They can be either reflexive or reciprocal, meaning either "self" or "each other":

*Ils **se** parlent.* → They are talking to themselves, OR They are talking to each other.

If the meaning is not clear, there are words that can be added, especially *l'un(e) (à) l'autre, les un(e)s les autres:*

*Ils **se** regardent **les un(e)s les autres**. Ils **se** parlent **les un(e)s aux autres**.*
(D.O.)   (I.O.)

NOTE:

1. We use many more reflexives in French than in English because transitive verbs must have objects. Contrast:

   Nous arrêtons l'auto. → We stop the car.
   *Nous **nous** arrêtons.* → We stop.

2. Some French verbs are only reflexive. Use the reflexive pronoun in French, but do not translate it:

   *Je **m'en** vais.* → I'm leaving.
   *Ils **s'amusent**.* → They are having a good time.

Disjunctive Pronouns in English

WHAT ARE THEY? Disjunctive pronouns are not attached to a verb (disjunctive means "not joined"). They are used alone or as an extra word to give special emphasis, to intensify the impression.

WHAT FORMS AND USES DO THEY HAVE? The forms of these pronouns depend on the use:

1. Used alone, the disjunctive pronoun is put in the subjective case, if required, in formal English and in the objective case for informal use:

   *Who's there? **I** (formal; "I am" is understood) OR **Me** (informal).*

2. As an intensifier, the reflexive pronoun is usually used:

   *I'll do it **myself**! He told me so **himself**.*

3. Sometimes we merely raise our voices to be more emphatic:

   ***You** do it!*

Disjunctive Pronouns in French

WHAT FORMS DO THEY HAVE? The disjunctive pronouns have special forms in French.

Person	Singular	Plural
1	moi	nous
2	toi	vous
3	lui, elle, soi (oneself)	eux, elles

WHAT USES DO THEY HAVE?

1. Use alone: *Qui est là? **Moi!***

2. Use as a complement after *c'est: C'est **toi!***

3. Use an an intensifier: ***Moi,** je vais le faire* or *Je vais le faire, **moi.*** (*I'm* going to do it.)

4. Use with *même* for emphasis: *Il me l'a dit **lui-même.*** (He told me so *himself.*)

5. Use after prepositions or conjunctions:

   ***Après nous,** le déluge.* (Madame de Pompadour)
   *Paul est plus grand **que toi.***
   *Chacun **pour soi.*** (Every man for himself.)

6. Use for compound subjects: ***Jean et moi,** nous y allons.*

7. Use with affirmative commands: *Donnez-**moi** votre billet.*

Relative Pronouns in English

WHAT ARE THEY? Relative pronouns are words that begin a relative clause. They replace a noun called the antecedent and usually come directly after that noun.

WHAT FORMS DO THEY HAVE?

	Subject	Object	Possessive	Indirect Object/Obj. of Prep.
Person	who (that)	whom (that)	whose	to (by) whom
Thing	which (that)	which (that)	whose (of which)	to (by) which where (for place prepositions) when (for time words)

To find the correct pronoun, you must know:

1. whether the antecedent is a person or a thing.
2. the function of the pronoun in the clause.
3. for subjects and objects, whether the clause is restrictive or nonrestrictive.

   A **restrictive** clause defines the noun. Choose *that* and do not set the clause off by commas:

   *The book **that** you just read is world-renowned.*

   Without the clause, you would not know which book was meant. It is an essential definition.

   A **nonrestrictive** clause describes the noun rather than defining it. It is not necessary in the sentence. Choose *who, whom,* or *which* and set the clause off by commas:

   *Madame Bovary, **which** the class is going to read, is very famous.*

   You could eliminate the relative clause and the sentence would still make sense. It is a nonessential description.

WHAT USES DO THEY HAVE?

1. Relative pronouns introduce clauses that give additional information about the antecedent.
2. They allow you to join two short sentences for smoothness and to avoid repetition:
   Mrs. Dubois came yesterday. Mrs. Dubois is an expert pianist.
   *Mrs. Dubois, **who** is an expert pianist, came yesterday.*
3. They can be subjects, direct objects, indirect objects, possessives, or objects of a preposition in the relative clause.
4. Relative pronouns are inflected only for case, not person or number. Their form depends on their function in the clause.

NOTE: The function of the antecedent in the main clause has no effect on the choice of pronoun.

Relative Pronouns in French

WHAT FORMS DO THEY HAVE?

	Subject	Object	Object of Preposition	Other
Person	qui	que	qui / lequel	dont
Thing	qui	que	*a form of* lequel	dont où (*where* or *when*)

NOTE: Remember to use contractions with *à* and *de*, e.g., *duquel*. See p. 77.

Unlike English, French does not use different pronouns to distinguish between restrictive and nonrestrictive clauses:

*Le livre **que** vous venez de lire est célèbre dans le monde entier.*
*Madame Bovary, **que** la classe va lire, est très célèbre.*

Relative pronouns are often omitted in English:

That's the man I saw yesterday!

French does not allow that:

*C'est l'homme **que** j'ai vu hier.*

All relative pronouns must have antecedents. If there isn't one, you must supply *ce:*

He didn't come, which (subject) *surprised me.*

There is no word to serve as an antecedent for *which*, therefore we say:

*Il n'est pas venu, **ce qui** m'a surpris.*

If the relative pronoun had been *que* or *dont*, you would have used *ce que* or *ce dont*.

Relative pronouns can take any form of the verb. This is true in English too, but many people do not practice this:

*C'est moi **qui suis** anxieux.* → It is I who am worried.
*Ce sont nous **qui arrivons.*** → We are the ones who are coming.

This can cause problems because relative pronouns (in both English and French) often look the same as interrogatives (*who?*, *what?*, etc.), and these always take a third person verb:

*Qui **est** anxieux? Moi.* → Who is worried? I am.
*Qui **arrive**? Nous.* → Who is coming? We are.

How to Analyze Relative Pronouns in English

Mr. Smith is an excellent **cook.**   **Mr. Smith** made these **pies.**
(subject)   (complement)   (subject)   (direct object)

1. Find the repeated element → *Mr. Smith.*

2. Find the function of the repeated element in the second sentence, which will become the relative clause → *subject.*

3. Choose the relative pronoun → *who* (person, subject).

4. Copy the first sentence through the antecedent → *Mr. Smith...*

5. Put in the correct relative pronoun, in this case, *who* → *Mr. Smith, who...*

6. Copy the relative clause → *Mr. Smith, who made these pies...*

7. Copy the rest of the first sentence. Leave out any parts represented by the relative pronoun → *Mr. Smith, who made these pies, is an excellent cook.*

Other examples:

The ten books are on the table. I am reading them.
The ten books that I am reading are on the table.

We use *that* because:

1. It is the object of "am reading" in the clause (no commas).

2. It refers to a thing.

3. It is restrictive (defines which ten books).

Mr. Jones died today. I saw him yesterday.
Mr. Jones, whom I saw yesterday, died today.

We use *whom* because:

1. It is the object of "I saw" (with commas).

2. It refers to a person.

3. It is nonrestrictive. (You know who Mr. Jones is. This merely gives an extra fact.)

The student is asleep. I am speaking to that student.
The student to whom I am speaking is asleep.

We use *to whom* because:

1. It is the indirect object (with no commas).

2. It refers to a person.

3. It is restrictive.

The old house is falling down. I lived in that house as a child.
The old house where (in which) I lived as a child is falling down.

We use *where* because:

1. It replaces a place preposition plus noun object (no commas).

2. It refers to a thing. (*In which* is also correct.)

*How to Analyze
Relative Pronouns
in English
(continued)*

*The woman lives in New York. I took her coat.
The woman whose coat I took lives in New York.*

We use *whose* because:

1. It is possessive (no commas).

2. It refers to a person.

3. It is restrictive.

How to Analyze Relative Pronouns in French

The important considerations are *function in the clause* and *word order:*

M. Smith *est un excellent* **chef.**		**M. Smith** *a fait ces* **tartes.**	
(subject)	(complement)	(subject)	(direct object)

1. Find the repeated element → *M. Smith.*

2. Find the function of the repeated element in the second sentence, which will become the relative clause → *subject.*

3. Choose the relative pronoun → *qui.*

4. Copy the first sentence through the noun phrase to be described → *M. Smith...*

5. Put in the relative pronoun (with preposition, if any) to replace *M. Smith* → *qui.*

6. Copy the rest of the second sentence (now a relative clause) → *M. Smith, qui a fait ces tartes...*

7. Copy any other parts of the first sentence → *M. Smith, qui a fait ces tartes, est un excellent chef.*

Try it with other sentences. Follow the same steps until they seem natural.

*Les dix livres sont sur la table. Je les lis.
Les dix livres que je lis sont sur la table.*

*M. Jones est mort aujourd'hui. Je l'ai vu hier.
M. Jones, que j'ai vu hier, est mort aujourd'hui.*

*L'étudiant est endormi. Je parle à cet étudiant.
L'étudiant à qui je parle est endormi.*

*La vieille maison s'écroule. Je vivais dans cette maison dans ma jeunesse.
La vieille maison où je vivais dans ma jeunesse s'écroule.* (*Dans laquelle* is also possible.)

*La dame habite à New York. J'ai pris le manteau de cette dame.
La dame dont j'ai pris le manteau habite à New York.*

This may seem complicated, requiring a lot of thought. That is because many people use short sentences when speaking. Relative clauses are used mainly to vary your written style—when you have time to think, cross something out and write it in a different way.

Demonstrative Pronouns in English

WHAT ARE THEY? Demonstrative pronouns are words that point out someone or something.

WHAT FORMS DO THEY HAVE? There are only four forms for the demonstratives:

Singular	Plural
this (one)	these
that (one)	those

WHAT USES DO THEY HAVE? They distinguish only between what is near (this, these) and far (that, those) and between singular and plural. No changes are made for gender or case:

I can't decide which of the chairs to buy.
***This one** is lovely, but **that one** is comfortable.*
***This** is lovely, but **that** is comfortable.*

Demonstrative Pronouns in French

WHAT FORMS DO THEY HAVE?

Gender	Singular	Plural
Masculine	celui	ceux
Feminine	celle	celles

WHAT USES DO THEY HAVE? Demonstrative pronouns replace a demonstrative adjective plus its noun:

> *ce monsieur (**cet homme**)* → ***celui***
> *cette dame (**cette image**)* → ***celle***
> *ces hommes* → ***ceux***
> *ces dames* → ***celles***

In French, demonstrative pronouns are never used by themselves. Something must follow to explain them. This may be:

1. **-ci** or **-là.** These distinguish between near (*-ci*) and far (*-là*):

   Ceux-ci *sont bons, mais **ceux-là** sont meilleurs.* → These are good, but those are better.

   They are also used for *former* and *latter*. The one "nearest" to your words is the last one mentioned. Therefore **celui-ci** is the *latter* and **celui-là** is the *former:*

   *Voilà John et Marc. **Celui-ci** (Marc) est français, mais **celui-là** (John) est américain.*

2. a **prepositional phrase:**

   *Voici ma composition et **celle de Marie**.* → Here is my composition and Mary's.

3. a **relative clause:**

   *Voici **celui que j'aime**.* → Here is the one I like.

✔ QUICK CHECK

Notice that the form of the demonstrative pronoun is made up of the pronoun *ce* plus the **disjunctive pronoun** that would be used for that noun:

Demonstrative Adjective + Noun	Disjunctive Pronoun	Demonstrative Pronoun
ce monsieur	lui	celui
cette dame	elle	celle
ces étudiants	eux	ceux
ces étudiantes	elles	celles

Interrogative Pronouns in English

WHAT ARE THEY? Interrogative pronouns are those used to ask a question.

WHAT FORMS DO THEY HAVE? Interrogative pronouns have different forms for people and things. The pronoun referring to people, *who,* is also inflected for case.

	People	**Things**
Subject	who?	which?
		what?
Object	whom?	which?
		what?

No change is made for number. *Who?* or *what?* can refer to one or more than one.

WHAT USES DO THEY HAVE?

1. Person, subject   **Who** *is coming? John* OR *The Smiths.*
2. Thing, subject   **What** *is going on? A riot.*
3. Person, direct object   **Whom** *did you see? John.*
4. Thing, direct object   **What** *are you doing? My homework.*
5. Person, indirect object*   **To whom** *are you speaking? To Mary.*
6. Person, object of preposition   **With whom** *are you going? With Jean-Luc.*
7. Thing, object of preposition   **What** *are you thinking* **about?** *About the music.*

Which? is an interrogative pronoun related to choice. It can simply be *which?,* used in the singular or plural, or *which one(s)?*

Here are two books. **Which (one)** *do you want?*
There are many good shops in town. **Which (ones)** *do you like best?*

Interrogative Pronouns in French

WHAT FORMS DO THEY HAVE? Interrogatives are confusing in both English and French because the same words are used for many things, but they are more complex in French because in most cases you have a choice of two forms.

A. SHORT FORMS

	Subject	Object	Object of Preposition
Person	qui	qui	qui
	Qui est là?	*Qui regardez-vous?*	*À qui parlez-vous?*
Thing	no form	que	quoi
		Que faites-vous?	*De quoi avez-vous besoin?*

*To or for indicate the indirect object. To review the indirect object, see p 18.

Interrogative Pronouns in French (continued)

B. LONG FORMS

These interrogatives are made up of three parts: *interrogative pronoun* + "*est-ce*" + *relative pronoun*. The first part tells you if it is a person or a thing; the last, if it is the subject or the object. The middle part, "est-ce," shows that the subject and verb will be in normal word order.

WHAT USES DO THEY HAVE?

1. Person, subject | *Qui arrive?* OR *Qui est-ce qui arrive? Jean* OR *Les Smith.*
2. Thing, subject | *Qu'est-ce qui arrive? Une émeute.*
3. Person, direct object | *Qui avez-vous vu? Qui est-ce que vous avez vu? Jean.*
4. Thing, direct object | *Que faites-vous? Qu'est-ce que vous faites? Mes devoirs.*
5. Person, indirect object | *À qui parlez-vous? À Marie.*
6. Person, object of prep. | *Avec qui allez-vous? Avec Jean-Luc.*
7. Thing, object of prep. | *À quoi pensez-vous? À la musique.*

✔ **QUICK CHECK**

	Interrogative Pronoun				Relative Pronoun
Person (Subject)	qui	+	est-ce	+	qui
Person (Object)	qui	+	est-ce	+	que
Thing (Subject)	qu'	+	est-ce	+	qui
Thing (Object)	qu'	+	est-ce	+	que

C. CHOICE INTERROGATIVES

Another kind of interrogative pronoun asks for a choice: *Which one(s)?* These forms agree in gender and number with the noun they replace.

They are straightforward as they are made up of the *definite article* + the *interrogative adjective.*

Gender	Singular	Plural
Masculine	lequel	lesquels
Feminine	laquelle	lesquelles

They are used to choose among more than one possibility:

*Voici deux livres. **Lequel** voulez-vous?*
*Il y a beaucoup de bonnes boutiques en ville. **Lesquelles** préférez-vous?*

ADJECTIVES

Introducing Adjectives in English

WHAT ARE THEY? See p. 10.

WHAT FORMS DO THEY HAVE? Some adjectives are invariable while others change form. These changes depend on the type of adjective. The types will be discussed separately below.

WHAT USES DO THEY HAVE? Primary uses of the adjective are:

1. as modifiers of nouns or pronouns.

2. as complements of either the subject or an object.

   Their function determines their position in the sentence:

1. As modifiers, the adjectives usually come before the nouns or pronouns:

   Buy **that small white** house (or the **blue** one).
       (adjectives)   (noun)   (adj.) (pronoun)

2. As modifiers of indefinite pronouns, the adjectives follow:

   Something **terrible** is happening.
   (indef. pro.) (adj.)

3. As a subject complement, the adjective follows the verb "to be" or the linking verb and describes the subject:

   Mrs. Duval is **happy.** They seem **pleased.**
         (to be)   (linking verb)

4. As an object complement, the adjective follows the direct object noun or pronoun:

   That made the exam **hard.** We considered him **crazy.**
         (noun) (adj.)   (pro.) (adj.)

WHAT KINDS ARE THERE? Each of the following will be discussed separately:

1. **Descriptive.**

2. **Proper** (a kind of descriptive adjective).

3. **Limiting** (includes **demonstratives, possessives, indefinites, interrogatives, numbers,** and **determiners**).

Introducing Adjectives in French

WHAT FORMS DO THEY HAVE? Adjectives in French agree in gender and number with the noun they modify. If an adjective describes a mixed group (masculine and feminine), then the adjective is masculine plural.

WHAT USES DO THEY HAVE? They are used, as in English, as modifiers or complements, but their position in the sentence is different. See p. 49.

Descriptive Adjectives in English

WHAT ARE THEY? Descriptive adjectives describe a noun or pronoun.

WHAT FORMS DO THEY HAVE? Many of them may be inflected to show comparison.

Descriptive Adjectives in French

WHAT FORMS DO THEY HAVE? Descriptive adjectives normally add "-e" for the feminine and "-s" for the plural. The masculine singular form is the one listed first in vocabularies and dictionaries:

Gender	Singular	Plural
Masculine	grand	grand**s**
Feminine	grand**e**	grand**es**

There are, however, several groups of adjectives with irregular forms (note the corresponding examples in the table on p. 49):

1. Adjectives ending in mute "-e" in the masculine do not add another "-e" for the feminine.
2. Adjectives ending in "-s" or "-x" do not add "-s" for the plural.
3. Adjectives ending in "-eux" become "-euse" in the feminine and do not change for the masculine plural.
4. Adjectives ending in "-f" become "-ve" in the feminine.
5. Adjectives ending in "-eil," "-el," "-il," "-ien," and "-on" double the consonant before adding "-e."
6. Adjectives ending in "-ier" change to "-ière" in the feminine.
7. Adjectives ending in "-al" change to "-aux" in the masculine plural.
8. Some adjectives have an alternative masculine form to use before words beginning with a vowel and many words beginning with "h" to make pronunciation easier. The feminine is formed from the alternative masculine.
9. Some are completely irregular.

Descriptive Adjectives in French (continued)

Types	Masculine	Feminine	Masculine Plural	Feminine Plural
1	facile	facile	faciles	faciles
2	français	française	français	françaises
3	heureux	heureuse	heureux	heureuses
4	vif	vive	vifs	vives
5	bon	bonne	bons	bonnes
6	fier	fière	fiers	fières
7	familial	familiale	familiaux	familiales
8	vieux (vieil)	vieille	vieux	vieilles
	fou (fol)	folle	fous	folles
	beau (bel)	belle	beaux	belles
9	blanc	blanche	blancs	blanches

WORD ORDER. Normally, descriptive adjectives in French follow the noun. First, you say what you are talking about (*une maison*), then you describe it (*une maison blanche*). But, some common adjectives are placed before the noun: *une grande maison, une petite voiture.*

Most adjectives of this kind fit into one of four groups (along with their opposites): Size, Handsomeness, Age, Goodness (SHAG):

S	**Size**	court	long
		grand	petit
		haut	bas
		gros	mince
H	**Handsomeness**	beau / joli	laid / vilain
A	**Age**	vieux	jeune
G	**Goodness**	bon	mauvais / méchant
			pauvre (*pitiful, not penniless*)

NOTE: Some adjectives, including some of the above, can change position. If they are meant literally, they tend to follow the noun; figurative meanings precede the noun:

*un **grand** homme* → a great man
*un **homme** grand* → a tall man
*une **ancienne** église* → a former church
*une **église** ancienne* → an old church
*un **pauvre** homme* → a man to be pitied
*un **homme** pauvre* → a man with no money
*une **chère** amie* → a dear friend
*une **robe** chère* → an expensive dress

Comparison of Adjectives in English

The three degrees of comparison are:

positive—comparative—superlative

1. Regular comparisons add "-er" and "-est" to short adjectives:

    *short, short**er**, short**est***
    *pretty, pretti**er**, pretti**est***

2. Longer adjectives are compared by using *more* and *most,* or the negatives *less* and *least:*

    *determined, **more** determined, **most** determined*
    *obvious, **less** obvious, **least** obvious*

3. Some adjectives have irregular comparisons:

    good, better, best
    bad, worse, worst

4. Adjectives that cannot be compared include absolutes, which are by definition superlative:

    unique, perfect

    Uniqueness and perfection cannot be brought to a higher degree.

5. When a comparison is made, the following words introduce the second element:

    *He is taller **than** I (am).* (comparative)
    *He is the tallest boy **in** the class. He is the tallest **of** all of my students.* (superlative)

If an adjective is already in the comparative, do not add *more* to it. Greater contrast may be expressed with words like *much:*

much *smaller,* **much** *more difficult*

Comparison of Adjectives in French

1. Regular French adjectives form the comparative with **plus** (*more*), **aussi** (*as*, in the sense of equal), or **moins** (*less*) plus the adjective:

   grand, **plus** *grand,* **aussi** *grand,* **moins** *grand*

2. Superlatives are formed with the correct definite article plus the comparative (*le plus grand, la moins petite,* etc.):

   un **grand** *garçon* → *un* **plus grand** *garçon* → **le plus grand** *garçon*
   un bus **rapide** → *un bus* **moins rapide** → *le bus* **le moins rapide**

   NOTE: The adjective remains in the same position whether it is positive, comparative, or superlative:

   J'achète une **grande** *maison.*
   J'achète une **plus grande** *maison.*
   J'achète **la plus grande** *maison de la ville.*

3. The most common irregular comparisons are:

   bon, meilleur, le meilleur
   mauvais, pire, le pire

4. Adjectives that cannot be compared include absolutes, which are by definition superlative:

   unique, parfait

   Since uniqueness and perfection cannot be brought to a higher degree, we cannot use *le (la, les) plus* with them.

5. When a comparison is made between two elements, use *que* or *de* to link them:

   Jean est plus grand **que** *Marie.* (comparative)
   Marie est la plus grande **de** *sa famille.* (superlative)

✔ QUICK CHECK

Comparative construction: (1) les hommes, (2) les femmes, (3) être intelligents:

Noun 1	+	Verb	+	Comp.	+	Adjective	+	Que	+	Noun 2
Les hommes		*sont*		*plus*		*intelligents*		*que*		*les femmes.*
				aussi						
				moins						

Superlative construction: (1) Carole, (2) la classe, (3) être diligent:

Noun 1	+	Verb	+	Comp.	+	Adjective	+	De	+	Noun 2
Carole		*est*		*la plus*		*diligente*		*de*		*la classe.*

Be careful that the adjective always agrees with the noun or pronoun it describes.

Proper Adjectives in English

Proper adjectives are a type of descriptive adjective formed from a proper noun (see p. 16):

Noun	Adjective
Rome	*Roman*
Shakespeare	*Shakespearian*

In English, both proper nouns and their adjectives are capitalized. Sometimes you cannot tell them apart by their form:

Noun	Adjective
the French	*the French people*

Limiting Adjectives in English

Limiting adjectives do not add to your knowledge of the noun, but they do direct you toward the right one by limiting the choices:

this *chapter* (not another one), ***his*** *book* (not hers), ***some*** *people* (but not others), ***whose*** *coat?* (limits the answer to a person), *the **second** lesson* (not the first)

Under the heading of limiting adjectives, demonstratives, possessives, interrogatives, indefinites, and others need to be discussed separately.

Proper Adjectives in French

Proper adjectives are formed from proper nouns in French, but they are not capitalized:

Noun	Adjective
un Français	*le peuple français*

Limiting Adjectives in French

See the discussion under the English forms.

Demonstrative Adjectives in English

WHAT ARE THEY? Demonstrative adjectives point out which of a group is (are) the one(s) that you are referring to.

WHAT FORMS DO THEY HAVE? They have the same forms as the demonstrative pronouns (see p. 40) and distinguish in the same way between near and far and between singular and plural:

	Singular	Plural
Near	this	these
Far	that	those

No agreement is needed for person, gender, or case. The demonstrative adjective precedes its noun:

This woman is talking to that man.
These little boys hate those dogs.

Demonstrative Adjectives in French

WHAT FORMS DO THEY HAVE? Demonstrative adjectives agree with the noun they modify in gender and number:

Gender	Singular	Plural
Masculine	ce (cet)	ces
Feminine	cette	ces

WHAT USES DO THEY HAVE? The near/far distinction made in English does not appear unless there is a possibility of confusion. Then *-ci* or *-là* must be added to the noun to distinguish:

Cette femme parle à cet homme.
Ces petits garçons détestent ces chiens-là.

Possessive Adjectives in English

WHAT ARE THEY? Possessive adjectives modify a noun by telling to whom or what it belongs.

WHAT FORMS DO THEY HAVE? They tell the person, number, and gender (in the third person singular) of the *possessor* (the one who owns):

Person	Singular	Plural
1	my	our
2	your	your
3	his, her	their
	its, one's	

The adjectives do not tell us anything about the person or thing that is possessed:

Mr. Dupont's son → *his son* (third person, masculine, singular)
Mrs. Dupont's son → *her son* (third person, feminine, singular)
the Duponts' son → *their son* (third person, plural)

WHAT USES DO THEY HAVE? The possessive adjective is always used with the noun:

my mother, *our* child, *your* turn

If you wish to omit the noun, you must use a pronoun, e.g., *mine, ours, yours* (see p. 30).

Interrogative Adjectives in English

WHAT ARE THEY? Interrogative adjectives ask a question about limitation.

WHAT FORMS DO THEY HAVE?

1. Subjective and objective: which?, what?
2. Possessive: whose?

They are invariable, although they represent case.

WHAT USES DO THEY HAVE?

1. To ask a question:
   What assignment is for today? (subject)
   Which class do you have at 10? (object)
   Whose coat is this? (possessive)
2. As an exclamation:
   What a pretty house! *What* a job!

Possessive Adjectives in French

Possessives are adjectives, so they agree in gender and number with the noun they modify, NOT with the person who is the owner.

WHAT FORMS DO THEY HAVE?

	Person	Masculine	Feminine	Plural	English Equivalent
Singular	1	mon	ma	mes	my
	2	ton	ta	tes	your
	3	son	sa	ses	his, her, its
Plural	1	notre	notre	nos	our
	2	votre	votre	vos	your
	3	leur	leur	leurs	their

This is quite different from English. *Son cahier* can mean either *his notebook* or *her notebook. Son,* the masculine form, is used because *cahier* is masculine. For instance, Anne can say:

*Voici **mon** cahier, **ma** traduction et **mes** exercices.*

Anne does not have a different gender or number, but the three things she possesses in this sentence do.

NOTE: Feminine singular nouns beginning with a vowel or mute "h" take *mon, ton,* and *son:*

mon *ami* and **mon** *amie*

Mon is used in both cases because *amie* begins with a vowel. Notice too that they sound the same. As long as you are speaking and not writing, you give nothing away.

Interrogative Adjectives in French

WHAT FORMS DO THEY HAVE? These adjectives are inflected for gender and number. They agree with the noun they modify:

	Masculine	Feminine
Singular	quel	quelle
Plural	quels	quelles

These adjectives present little difficulty as long as they appear directly before the noun. However, when they are separated by the verb, it is harder for speakers of English to recognize them as adjectives.

WHAT USES DO THEY HAVE?

1. To ask a question:

   ***Quel** est le devoir pour aujourd'hui?*
   ***Quel** cours avez-vous à 10 h.?*

Whose does not exist as an interrogative adjective in French and requires a different construction.

2. As an exclamation:

   ***Quelle** jolie maison! **Quel** travail!*

Indefinite Adjectives in English

WHAT ARE THEY? Indefinite adjectives refer to nouns or pronouns that will not be defined more specifically:

Some students learn fast.
Both lectures are at 10.
I want *another* pen.

Any girl will tell you.
Each (or *every*) class has its value.
Such behavior is terrible.

WHAT FORMS DO THEY HAVE? These adjectives are invariable, i.e., they do not change their form. Some, however, may be used only with singular nouns (*each, every, another*); some only with plural ones (*both, other*); and some with either singular or plural (e.g., *some: some coffee, some people*).

Other Limiting Adjectives in English

A. ORDINAL NUMBERS

Show the order in which things come. One, two, three (and all numbers ending in one, two, and three, except eleven, twelve, thirteen) have irregular ordinals:

first, second, third, etc.

All others form the ordinal by adding "-th": *fourth, ninth, sixteenth,* etc.

B. DETERMINERS

Determiners are often classified as adjectives (see p. 20).

Other Adjectival Forms in English

Many other kinds of words—even though they are not adjectives themselves—may be used as adjectives (i.e., to describe a noun or pronoun):

a *philosophy* professor (noun)
running water (present participle of a verb)
the *required* reading (past participle of a verb)
the poster *on the wall* (prepositional phrase)
the poster *that I bought* (relative clause)
I wondered what *to do.* (infinitive)
People *from all around* love him. (adverbial phrase)

Indefinite Adjectives in French

Quelques *étudiants apprennent vite.*
Les deux *conférences sont à 10 heures.*
Je voudrais un *autre* *stylo.*

N'importe quelle *fille vous le dira.*
Chaque *cours a ses mérites.*
De *telle* *conduite est répréhensible.*

Indefinite adjectives agree with their noun in gender and number just as descriptive adjectives do.

Other Limiting Adjectives in French

A. ORDINAL NUMBERS

Ordinal numbers are fairly easy in French. For the most part, merely add *-ième* to the number.

1. *Premier (-ière)* is irregular.
2. Some others have slight spelling adjustments:
    a. If the number ends in "-e," drop it → *quatre / quatrième.*
    b. Final "-f" changes to "-v" → *neuf / neuvième.*
    c. Final "-q" changes to "-qu" → *cinq / cinquième.*
3. "-ième" is often abbreviated as "e" above the line, e.g., **5ᵉ**.

B. DETERMINERS (See p. 21.)

Other Adjectival Forms in French

un professeur *de philosophie* (noun phrase)
l'eau *courante* (present participle)
la lecture *requise* (past participle)
l'affiche *au mur* (prepositional phrase)
l'affiche *que j'ai achetée* (relative clause)
Je me suis demandé que *faire.* (infinitive)
Des gens *de partout* *l'aiment.* (adverb)

CHAPTER SIX

ADVERBS

Introducing Adverbs in English

WHAT ARE THEY? See p. 11.

WHAT FORMS DO THEY HAVE? Adverbs formed from descriptive adjectives most frequently end in "-ly."

*active, active**ly***   *slow, slow**ly***

1. Like adjectives, adverbs may be inflected to show comparison:

Positive	Comparative	Superlative
actively	more actively	most actively
actively	less actively	least actively

The comparative is used to show the similarity or differences between how two people or things do something, or degrees of difference in qualifying an adjective or adverb. The superlative compares more than two. There must also be a word to tie the two points of comparison together:

*I walk **slowly.** (positive)*
*John walks **more slowly than** I do. (comparative)*
*Monica walks **the most slowly of** all. (superlative)*

2. Some adverbs not ending in "-ly" may take "-er" and "-est," like adjectives:

*He runs fast, but I run **faster.***   *Mary runs the **fastest** of all.*

3. Some adverbs form their comparison irregularly:

well, better, best
badly, worse, worst

WHAT USES DO THEY HAVE?

1. Adverbs answer the questions *how, when, where,* or *how much* about a verb, an adjective, or another adverb. Sometimes a phrase takes the place of a single adverb:

Yesterday he came	**here** and	**very**	**quickly** told the story.
(when)	(where)	(how much)	(how)
This morning he went	**there**		**by car.**

(Continued on p. 64)

Introducing Adverbs in French

WHAT FORMS DO THEY HAVE? Most adverbs formed from descriptive adjectives add "-ment" to the feminine form of the adjective.

actif(ve), **activement** *lent(e),* **lentement**

1. Like adjectives, adverbs may show comparison:

Positive	Comparative	Superlative
activement	plus activement	le plus activement
	aussi activement	
	moins activement	le moins activement

The words used to link the two elements being compared are the same as for adjectives. (See
✔ **Quick Check,** p. 51. The same pattern will work for adverbs.)

*Je marche **lentement.*** (positive)
*Jean marche **plus lentement que** moi.* (comparative)
*Jean marche **le plus lentement de** tous.* (superlative)

2. Some of the most common adverbs do not end in "-ment." They must be learned as vocabulary. They are compared in the same way as others:

*Il court **vite,** mais je cours **plus vite.** Marie court **le plus vite** de tous.*

3. Two adverbs—*well* and *badly*—form their comparisons irregularly:

Positive	Comparative	Superlative
bien	mieux	le mieux
mal	pis (plus mal)	le pis (plus mal)

NOTE: These forms are easy to confuse with the adjectives *bon* (good) and *mauvais* (bad). It may help to remember that *bien* and *mieux* both have an "i" as the second letter and that the two three-letter words (*mal* and *pis*) go together.

WHAT USES DO THEY HAVE?

1. See the uses in English:

(when)	(where)	(how much)	(how)
Hier	*il est venu **ici***	*et a **très***	***vite** raconté l'histoire.*
Ce matin	*il **y** est allé*		***en voiture.***

(Continued on p. 65)

Introducing
Adverbs
in English
(continued)

2. **Negatives.** Some adverbs make a sentence negative. These include words like *not, nowhere, never.* In standard English we may not use two negative words in one sentence unless we wish to express a positive, not a negative idea:

*He doesn't have **no** friends, but he has **too few.***

The first clause used alone and intended as a negative would not be standard English. This includes not only negative adverbs, but nouns and adjectives as well.

3. **Questions.** Another group introduces questions: *when?, where?, how?, why?* These are the questions that the majority of adverbs answer with respect to the verb, but the interrogative words themselves are adverbs too:

***When** does he arrive? **How** do you know that?*

4. **Relative clauses.** The same adverbs that ask questions may also be used to form relative clauses. These clauses tell when, where, how, etc., the verb's action will take place and can be used in the same way:

*We are going to the movies **when we finish our work.***

ADJECTIVES VS. ADVERBS

To be sure of choosing the correct word, it is essential to ask yourself:

Am I *describing* some*one* (some*thing*)? → **adjective**
Am I *describing how* (*when, where, why*) something is *done*? → **adverb**

*The **poem** is **good**, and the poet **reads** it **well.***
(noun)   (adjective)   (verb)   (adverb)

*The **play** is **bad** and it's **badly performed.***
  (noun) (adjective)   (adverb)   (verb)

This is especially important for verbs of mental (or emotional) state, or sensory verbs, which can be followed by either an adjective or an adverb. One of the most common examples is:

*I feel **bad.*** (I am sick, unhappy, etc.)
*I feel **badly.*** (My hands are not sensitive.)

Introducing Adverbs in French (continued)

2. **Negatives** can be a problem in French for two reasons: They have two parts, and more than one can be used in a sentence.

a. *Ne . . . pas* is the English "not." *Ne* goes before the verb in a simple tense and *pas* after it. For the perfect (compound) tenses, the auxiliary, which agrees with the subject, is treated like the simple-tense verb.

NOTE: When the verb form and its subject are joined by a hyphen, they are considered one word and can't be broken up. Both *ne* and *pas* precede an infinitive:

*Je n'aime **pas** Pierre.* ***Ne** travaillez-vous **pas**?*
*Nous **ne** sommes **pas** encore arrivés. **N'**est-elle **pas** arrivée?*
*Je commence à **ne pas** comprendre.*

b. There are other, more specific negative adverbs. These words replace *pas:*

ne . . . jamais (never)   *ne . . . plus* (no longer)   *ne . . . point* (not at all)
ne . . . ni . . . ni (neither . . . nor) to contrast nouns, adjectives, adverbs, etc.
ne . . . ni . . . ne (neither . . . nor) to contrast verbs

*Je n'aime **point** Pierre. **Ne** travaillez-vous **jamais**?*

With *ne . . . ni,* remember that *ne* goes before verbs (as with *ne . . . pas*) and *ni* before other parts of speech:

*Je **ne** vois **ni** Jean **ni** Pierre.* → I see neither John nor Peter.
*Il **ne** lit **ni ne** comprend le chinois.* → He neither reads nor understands Chinese.

Personne (no one) and *rien* (nothing, anything) are negative words, but they are pronouns, not adverbs, so they come in the subject or object position in the sentence. Their *ne* remains before the verb:

***Personne ne** fait **rien**!* → No one is doing anything!
*Je **n'**ai vu **personne**.* → I saw no one.

c. You can heap up negatives in French—which you can't do in standard English:

*Non! Je **ne** dis **plus jamais rien à personne**!*
No! I never tell anyone anything anymore.

With compound verbs, *rien* comes in the adverbial position:

*Je **n'**ai **rien** vu.*

d. *Ne . . . que* (only) is not negative, but it has a negative form. Remember to put the *que* before the word it modifies:

*Je **n'**ai **qu'**un frère.* → I have only one brother.
*Je **ne** l'ai appris **qu'**aujourd'hui.* → I found out only today.

3. **Questions:**

***Quand** arrive-t-il?* ***Comment** savez-vous cela?*

4. **Relative clauses:**

*Nous allons au cinéma **quand nous terminerons notre travail**.*

ADJECTIVES VS. ADVERBS

*Le **poème** est **bon**, et le poète le **lit bien**.*
     (noun)   (adj.)   (verb) (adverb)

*Le **pièce** est **mauvaise**, et on la **joue mal**.*
     (noun)   (adjective)   (verb) (adverb)

CHAPTER SEVEN

CONJUNCTIONS

Introducing Conjunctions in English

WHAT ARE THEY? See p. 11.

WHAT FORMS DO THEY HAVE? Conjunctions are function words; they are invariable.

WHAT KINDS ARE THERE? All conjunctions are linking words, but what is linked and the relationship between the linked parts determine to which of the three principal kinds of conjunctions a given one belongs: **coordinating, subordinating,** or **adverbial.**

WHAT USES DO THEY HAVE?

1. **Coordinating conjunctions** link two equal elements with the same grammatical construction. The two elements may be single words, phrases, or entire clauses:

   John **and** Mary (nouns)
   to be **or** not to be (infinitives)
   We came, **but** he was not there. (independent clauses)

   NOTE: Words belonging to a subgroup of these conjunctions are called **correlatives.** These conjunctions occur in pairs:

   Both John **and** Mary are in the class.

2. **Subordinating conjunctions** do not join equal elements. One element is subordinated to the other. The conjunction introduces the subordinate clause (the one that cannot stand alone as a sentence):

   Although he is hurrying, he is late. (contrast)
   We speak French **when** the Dubois are here. (time)
   Because this course is easy, we all get A's. (cause)

   Notice that the main idea of the sentence is in the main (independent) clause. The subordinate clause tells about the time, way, cause, or conditions involved and may show a contrast. Notice also that the main clause need not come first. You could reverse the order of the clauses in the examples above without changing the meaning of the sentence.

   There is also a subgroup of **correlative subordinating conjunctions.** Some of these are *if . . . then, so . . . that,* etc.:

   That course is so hard **that** many fail.

3. **Adverbial conjunctions** are sometimes called **conjunctive adverbs.** You can see from the names that grammarians are not sure whether they are really adverbs or conjunctions. Words or phrases like *therefore, perhaps, also, for example, as a result,* and *in other words,* fall into this category.

Introducing Conjunctions in French

WHAT USES DO THEY HAVE?

1. Coordination:

*Jean **et** Marie* (nouns)
*être **ou** ne pas être* (infinitives)
*Nous sommes venus, **mais** il n'était pas là.* (independent clauses)

Correlatives:

***Et** Jean **et** Marie sont dans la classe.*

2. Subordination:

***Bien qu'**il se dépêche, il est en retard.* (contrast)
*Nous parlons français **quand** les Dupont sont ici.* (time)
***Parce que** ce cours est facile, nous avons tous des "A."* (cause)

Correlative subordinates:

*Ce cours est **si** difficile **que** beaucoup d'étudiants échouent.*

3. Adverbial conjunctions:

donc, peut-être, par exemple, etc.

CHAPTER
EIGHT

INTERJECTIONS

Introducing Interjections in English

WHAT ARE THEY? See p. 11.

WHAT FORMS DO THEY HAVE? Interjections are normally invariable vocabulary items.

WHAT USES DO THEY HAVE? They are exclamations, often merely a sound (e.g., *ow!*), which are meant to convey emotion. They have no grammatical connection with the other words in the sentence. Set them off by commas.

Introducing Interjections in French

Interjections present no problems in French. They are merely vocabulary items. Some of the common ones are:

Aïe! Heu! Hein! Hélas!

CHAPTER NINE

PREPOSITIONS

Introducing Prepositions in English

WARNING! Prepositions, in any language, are very tricky words. Most of them have a basic meaning, but when they are used with other words, everything changes. You may think, for example, that you know what "up" means. Now consider the sentence:

*First he cut the tree **down,** the he cut it **up.***

Foreigners learning English would be confused by that sentence. And it is not an isolated example. Take the case of a friend calling John's house early in the morning and asking for him. John's wife replies:

*He'll be **down** as soon as he's **up.***

In other words, after learning a preposition, one must always be on the alert to see *how it is used* with other words. Often the meanings of one preposition will take several large pages of a good foreign language dictionary.

WHAT ARE THEY? See p. 11.

WHAT FORMS DO THEY HAVE? Prepositions are function words; they are invariable. They can be a single word or a group of words: *by, in spite of.*

WHAT USES DO THEY HAVE? Prepositions join a noun or pronoun (their object) to other words in the sentence and show its relation to them. In theory—also in formal English—a preposition is followed immediately by its object:

***to** the store, **about** the subject*

In practice—and in informal English, especially for phrasal verbs—we often leave the preposition until the end of the sentence:

*What is she waiting **for**?* INSTEAD OF ***For what** is she waiting?*
*This is the one that he is referring **to.*** INSTEAD OF *This is the one **to which** he is referring.*

Introducing Prepositions in French

WHAT FORMS DO THEY HAVE? French prepositions can be one or several words:

par (by), *à côté de* (beside)

They are invariable, except for *à* and *de*, which combine with the definite articles *le* and *les:*

Singular	Plural
à + le = au (m.)	à + les = aux (m.)
à + la = à la (f.)	à + les = aux (f.)
de + le = du (m.)	de + les = des (m.)
de + la = de la (f.)	de + les = des (f.)

NOTE: This combining takes place even if the *à* or *de* or the definite article is part of a longer word or expression:

à côté de + *le restaurant* = *à côté du restaurant*
près de ı *lequel* – *près duquel*

NOTE: Never expect a one-to-one equivalence between English and French prepositions. They are capricious in both languages.

In English you saw that the preposition comes before its object in formal speech and writing. In French (and many other languages) it must *nearly always* do so. Prepositions are not placed at the end of a sentence except in the most informal speech.

SOME SPECIAL PROBLEMS WITH PREPOSITIONS

1. With geographical names:

	Feminine "To"	Feminine "From"	Masculine "To"	Masculine "From"
Countries	en	de	à + *def. article*	de + *def. article*
Continents	en	de	none	none
States* and Provinces	en	de	dans + *def. article*	de + *def. article*
Cities**	à	de	à	de

* The states of the United States are masculine except for a few, well-known ones ending in "-e":

la Californie, la Floride, la Pennsylvanie, la Caroline du Nord, etc.

** If the name of the city contains a definite article, the article remains:

au Caire, à la Nouvelle-Orléans

(Continued on p. 78)

Introducing Prepositions in French (continued)

2. Verbs are often followed by infinitives. If two verbs are used to express a single thought, the *first* will determine whether any preposition (and which one) will be used to introduce a following infinitive. There can be more than two infinitives in a string (see the example below). In every case, if a verb is followed by an infinitive, the first of the two determines the preposition.

Here is a list of some verbs and the prepositions they take when followed by an infinitive:

à	de	none
avoir	choisir	savoir
aider	demander	devoir
réussir	décider	aller
chercher	dire	falloir
penser	essayer	vouloir
commencer (*usually*)	écrire	valoir
continuer	finir	croire
encourager	oublier	écouter
s'intéresser	permettre	entendre
jouer	refuser	regarder
inviter	regretter	pouvoir
se décider	suggérer	faire
apprendre	venir (de)	voir
se mettre		oser
		aimer
		laisser
		préférer
		sembler

*Je **vais** lire ce livre.* → I am going to read this book. (*aller* requires no preposition before an infinitive)

*Je **commence à** lire davantage.* → I am beginning to read more. (*commencer* takes *à* before an infinitive)

*J'**essaie de** commencer mon devoir.* → I am trying to start my assignment. (*essayer* takes *de*)

*Je **vais essayer de commencer à** lire ce livre.* → I am going to try to begin to read this book.

In each of the above cases it is the first of a group of any two that determines which preposition (if any) is to be used.

Verbs formed with prefixes usually require the same preposition as the basic verb:

*Je recommence **à** le faire.*
*Je promets **de** le faire.*

CHAPTER TEN

VERBS

INTRODUCING VERBS

WHAT ARE THEY? See p. 11.

WHAT FORMS DO THEY HAVE? English has fewer inflected verb forms than other European languages. Many verbs have only four forms, e.g., *talk/talks/talked/talking;* some have five, e.g., *sing/ sings/sang/sung/singing.*

In fact, in some systems of grammar, it is said that, technically, English has only two tenses—present and past—while other times are expressed by "periphrastic verbal constructions." This means that we use helping verbs and other expressions to convey differences. Here we will present verbs in a more traditional way, because it will help you to see the parallels between English and French constructions. Here are the principal parts of a verb:

Infinitive	Simple Past	Past Participle	Present Participle
talk	talked	talked	talking
sing	sang	sung	singing

Terms associated with verb forms are: **conjugation, tense, voice, transitive, intransitive,** and **mood.**

CONJUGATION has two meanings.

1. In Latin, and today in the Romance languages, verbs are classified into groups by their infinitive endings. English and German have only *regular* and *irregular,* sometimes called *weak* and *strong* verbs. Weak verbs take a regular ending to form the past: *talk/talked, follow/followed.* Strong verbs often change their vowel in the past or look completely different: *sing/sang, go/went.*

2. Conjugation also refers to a list, by person, of each possible form in a given tense. In Latin, there are six for every tense. The traditional example is *amare* (to love). Here is the present tense:

Person	Singular	Plural
1	amo I love	amamus we love
2	amas thou lovest	amatis you love
3	amat he loves	amant they love

Since each form is different, it is not even necessary to use a pronoun subject. The verb ending tells you who the subject is. The same is true for Spanish and Italian today.

In English we can conjugate verbs, but usually do not because there is only one inflected ending. We add an "-s" to the third person singular of the simple present tense:

Person	Singular	Plural
1	I speak	we speak
2	you speak	you speak
3	he (she) speaks	they speak

We need to have the pronoun (or a noun) with every verb form, because otherwise we would not know who or what the subject is.

TENSE comes from the Latin *tempus,* via the French *temps,* meaning "time." The tense tells you *when* something happened, *how long* it lasted, or whether it is *completed.*

VOICE can be either **active** or **passive.** Active voice means that the subject is or is doing something:

Mary is happy. Mary reads the newspaper. ("Mary" is the subject.)

Passive voice means that the subject is acted upon by an agent. The verb tells what happens to the subject:

The newspaper is read by Mary. ("Newspaper" is the subject.)

TRANSITIVE VERBS are ones that require an object to express a complete meaning:

Mr. White surprised a burglar.

Here, the verb, "surprised," is transitive because it takes an object, "burglar." If we left out the object, the sentence would not make sense. It would be incomplete.

INTRANSITIVE VERBS are ones that do not require an object:

Paul sat down.

Here, the verb, "sat," has no object; "down" is an adverb.

English has many verbs that can be either transitive or intransitive:

(subject)	(tr. verb)	(dir. obj.)	
Peter	**eats**	*dinner*	*at 7:00.*
The butcher	**weighs**	*the meat.*	

(subject)	(intr. verb)	
Peter	**eats**	*at 7:00.*
The butcher	**weighs**	*a lot.*

MOOD tells about the mood, or attitude, of the speaker. Is the speaker stating a fact? offering a possibility that has not happened yet? making a recommendation? giving an order? For these we use different moods. They are:

indicative, imperative, subjunctive

The indicative is by far the most common. The other two are used in special circumstances which you will learn.

Introducing Questions in English

There are four ways to form a question in English:

1. Place a question mark after a statement and raise your voice when saying it aloud:

   Anne is here already?
   That's Mark's idea?

2. Add a "tag," repeating the verb or auxiliary verb as a negative question. In English the tag changes depending on the subject and the verb:

   Peter is happy, isn't he?
   They came on time, didn't they?

3. Invert the subject and an *auxiliary* or *modal* verb, or the verb *to be:*

   Do you have any brothers?
   Is Pierre buying his books?
   Does Pierre buy his books?
   Has Pierre bought his books?
   May I see you this evening?
   Is Robert here today?

4. Use an interrogative word:

   Where is the library? When is the library open?

NOTE: At one time questions were often formed without an auxiliary, but that is less common now:

   Has Charles the book? has become *Does Charles have the book?*

Introducing Questions in French

There are four ways to form questions in French:

1. Place a question mark after a statement and raise your voice at the end when saying it aloud. This is usually limited to conversations (oral and written):

   Anne est déjà ici?
   C'est l'idée de Marc?

2. Place *n'est-ce pas* after any statement with which you expect your hearer or reader to agree:

   Pierre est content, n'est-ce pas?

3. Invert the pronoun subject and the verb. You do NOT need an auxiliary to form a question as you do in English:

   Avez-vous des frères?

   NOTE: Do not use inversion with *je*. That is very rare. Also, in the third person singular of "-er" verbs, add a "t" to make it easier to pronounce:

   Parlez-vous, but *parle-t-il, parle-t-elle, parle-t-on*

   When you have a noun subject, do not invert it with the verb. For example, make a question of *Pierre achète ses livres:*

   a. State the noun first: *Pierre ...*
   b. Invert the verb and the pronoun that would stand for Pierre (*il*): *Pierre achète-t-il ...*
   c. Complete the sentence: *Pierre achète-t-il ses livres?*
   d. You may begin the sentence with *est-ce que* and/or another interrogative word:

      Est-ce que la bibliothèque est ouverte? Où est la bibliothèque?
      Quand la bibliothèque est-elle ouverte? Quand est-ce que la bibliothèque est ouverte?

The above rules apply to any *simple* tense, i.e., one in which the verb is expressed by one word. In compound tenses (those that use two or more words to form the verb), treat the auxiliary verb in the same way as you did the simple tenses:

Avez-vous parlé?
Pierre a-t-il acheté ses livres?

WORD ORDER

With negatives: The verb-pronoun group is joined by a hyphen. A hyphenated group may NEVER be broken up. Therefore *ne ... pas* (or any other negative form) goes around the whole group:

Pierre n'a-t-il pas acheté ses livres?

With pronoun objects: As with statements, pronoun objects go directly before the verb in questions:

Les avez-vous?
Vous a-t-il vu?
Ne m'avez-vous pas vu?

With other kinds of questions: When you use intonation, *n'est-ce pas*, or *est-ce que* to ask a question, the word order remains exactly the same as for a statement. See the examples above.

Introducing Verbals in English

Verbals are forms of the verb that are not *finite,* i.e., do not agree with a subject and function as the predicate of a sentence. We will identify five kinds: **infinitive, past infinitive, gerund, present participle** (also called the **gerundive**), and **past participle.**

Present Infinitives in English

WHAT ARE THEY? The **present infinitive** is the basic form of the verb, the one you look up in a dictionary.

WHAT FORMS DO THEY HAVE? The infinitive is often identified by the word "to" preceding it. However, the "to" is omitted in many constructions, especially after verbs like *can* and *let.* Compare:

*I know how **to swim.***
*I can **swim.***

Both sentences contain the infinitive of "swim."

WHAT USES DO THEY HAVE? In addition to completing the verb, as in the above examples, infinitives may serve as subjects or objects of a sentence, as adjectives, or adverbs:

***To err** is human.* (subject)
*He hopes **to come** soon.* (object)
*English is the subject **to study**.* (adjective)
***To tell the truth,** he wants it more than ever.* (adverb)

Infinitives may also have their own direct objects and other modifiers:

*I am able **to do** that* (direct object) *easily* (adverb).

Past Infinitives in English

Past infinitives are formed with the present infinitive of the auxiliary (helping) verb and the past participle of the main verb.

to go (present infinitive) → *to have gone* (past infinitive)

They are used in the same ways as the present infinitive (see above):

***To have quit** is terrible.*

Gerunds in English

WHAT ARE THEY? Gerunds are often called verbal nouns.

Gerunds
in English
(continued)

WHAT FORMS DO THEY HAVE? Gerunds have the same functions as other nouns (see p. 14):

> ***Walking*** *is good for you.* (subject)
> *I like* ***singing.*** (object)

They may also have objects and modifiers:

> ***Making*** *money* (direct object) *quickly* (adverb) *is many people's goal.*

Introducing Verbals in French
Present Infinitives in French

WHAT FORMS DO THEY HAVE? French infinitives are grouped in three conjugations: those ending in "-er" (the most common), "-ir," and "-re."

WHAT USES DO THEY HAVE?

> ***Voir,*** *c'est* ***croire.*** (subject or complement)
> *Il souhaite* ***arriver*** *bientôt.* (object)
> *L'anglais, c'est le sujet à* ***étudier.*** (adjective)
> ***À vrai dire,*** *il le veut plus que jamais.* (adverb)
> *Pour bien* ***faire,*** *travaillez sérieusement.* (object of preposition)

NOTE: The prepositions *en* and *après* do not take a present infinitive. See below.

Infinitives may have objects (either nouns or pronouns) and be negated or otherwise modified:

> *Je veux* ***vous le montrer.*** (direct and indirect objects)
> *Je préfère* ***ne pas venir trop tôt.*** (negative precedes)

Past Infinitives in French

WHAT FORMS DO THEY HAVE? Past infinitives are formed as in English with the present infinitive of the auxiliary (*avoir* or *être*, depending on the verb) plus the past participle:

> *parler* → *avoir parlé*
> *aller* → *être allé*

NOTE: The past infinitive must be used with the preposition *après:*

> ***Après avoir mangé,*** *il est parti.*
> After eating (or having eaten), he left. After he ate, he left.

Gerunds in French

The infinitive is used as the verbal noun in French. See the first example above under present infinitives. They may be modified:

> ***Gagner vite*** *de l'argent, c'est le but de bien des gens.*

Participles in English

WHAT ARE THEY? They are verbal adjectives which constitute the third and fourth principal parts of a verb.

WHAT FORMS DO THEY HAVE?

1. **Present participles** end in "-ing":

   singing, talking, managing

2. **Past participles** end in "-ed" or "-n" for regular verbs:

   tried, gathered, concentrated, given

   For irregular verbs, the past participle is the third principal part. To find it, say: "Today I go; yesterday I went; I have gone." The form used after "I have" is the past participle. If you are not sure, look in the dictionary; the principal parts are given for every strong verb.

WHAT USES DO THEY HAVE? The two kinds of participles have basically the same uses:

1. As part of a compound verb (one requiring two or more words to form it):

   He **is talking.**
   They **have given.**

2. As adjectives:

   *a **talking** doll*
   *a **proven** fact*

3. In an absolute phrase:

   ***Walking** along the street, he met Robin.*
   Seen from the front, the building was even more imposing.

Participles in French

WHAT FORMS DO THEY HAVE?

1. **Present participles** end in "-ant." This ending is added to the first person plural of the present tense after dropping the "-ons":

   nous parlo̸n̸s̸ → **parlant**   *nous finisso̸n̸s̸* → **finissant**

   nous dormo̸n̸s̸ → **dormant**   *nous rendo̸n̸s̸* → **rendant**

   Three verbs are irregular in the present participle:

   être → **étant**   *avoir* → **ayant**   *savoir* → **sachant**

Participles
in French
(continued)

Remember that for all forms to keep the same consonant sounds as the infinitive, verbs ending in "-cer" and "-ger" also make a slight, but regular, change: "-cer" verbs put a cedilla under the "c"; "-ger" verbs add an "e" before any ending that begins with "o" or "a":

commençons → **commençant**   *mangeons* → **mangeant**

2. **Past participles** have different endings for the different conjugations, or groupings. Drop the infinitive ending "-er," "-ir," "-re," or "-oir" and add "-é," "-i," or "-u":

parler → **parlé**   *finir* → **fini**   *rendre* → **rendu**   *falloir* → **fallu**

There are a number of irregular past participles. Here are some of the most common:*

avoir = eu	faire = fait	venir = venu
voir = vu	dire = dit	mourir = mort
pouvoir = pu	écrire = écrit	
devoir = dû	mettre = mis	
recevoir = reçu	prendre = pris	
vouloir = voulu	être = été	
savoir = su	naître = né	
boire = bu		
croire = cru		
lire = lu		

WHAT USES DO THEY HAVE?

Present participles are used:

1. after the preposition *en* only to express "while doing something." All other prepositions are followed by an infinitive:

    En rentrant, *j'ai vu Paul.*

2. as an adjective. Adjectives ending in "-ant" were once verbals:

    un roseau **pensant** (Pascal: a thinking reed)

3. as an absolute modifying a noun or pronoun:

    Sachant *qu'il est difficile, j'évite M. Jones.*

Past participles:

1. *le premier* **venu** (noun; literally, the first one who came; means "just anybody")

2. *un fait* **prouvé** (adjective)

3. *j'ai* **parlé***; il aura* **fini** (second element of compound verb forms)

4. **Vu** *de face, le bâtiment était même plus imposant.* (absolute phrase)

---

* Compounds of verbs normally form their past participles in the same way as the basic verb:

mettre, remettre, promettre, etc. → **mis, remis, promis,** etc.

Indicative Mood

The verbs on pp. 88–109 are all in the **indicative** mood. It is the one used for stating facts or for making assertions as though they were facts.

Present Tenses in English

WHAT IS IT? The present tense is defined by its uses (see below).

WHAT FORMS DOES IT HAVE? Simple present, present progressive, or present emphatic.

1. **Simple present.** There is only one inflected form in the simple present. That is the third person singular, which adds "-s":

Person	Singular	Plural
1	I sing	we sing
2	you sing	you sing
3	he/she sings	they sing

2. **Present progressive.** This tense is formed with the present tense of *to be* plus the present participle:

Person	Singular	Plural
1	I am singing	we are singing
2	you are singing	you are singing
3	she is singing	they are singing

(Continued on p. 90)

Indicative Mood
Present Tense in French

Look at the explanation of the indicative mood in English.

WHAT FORMS DOES IT HAVE? French verbs in the present tense are easier than English in that they have only one form, not three. However, they are more difficult in that each conjugation is different and there are many more irregular verbs. One system of classifying irregular French verbs by the pattern of their conjugation can be found in Appendix III, p. 120.

1. "-er" verbs. Drop the infinitive ending (*-er*) and add *-e, -es, -e; -ons, -ez, -ent:*

Person	Singular	Plural
1	je parle	nous parlons
2	tu parles	vous parlez
3	il parle (elle/on/Jean)	ils parlent (elles/les Smith)

2. "-ir" verbs (type **finir**). Drop the *-ir* and add *-is, -is, -it; -issons, -issez, -issent:*

Person	Singular	Plural
1	je finis	nous finissons
2	tu finis	vous finissez
3	il/elle finit	ils/elles finissent

The above pattern is used for "-ir" verbs except those listed under *dormir* and some other irregular verbs. (See Appendix III, p. 120.)

"-ir" verbs (type **dormir**). Drop the *-ir* (and the final consonant in the singular) and add *-s, -s, -t; -ons, -ez, -ent:*

Person	Singular	Plural
1	je dors	nous dormons
2	tu dors	vous dormez
3	elle dort	ils dorment

Verbs like *dormir* are *partir, sortir, servir, mentir, courir,* and their compounds.

(Continued on p. 91)

Present
Tenses
in English
(continued)

3. Present emphatic. This tense is formed with the present tense of the verb *to do* plus the infinitive:

Person	Singular	Plural
1	I do sing	we do sing
2	you do sing	you do sing
3	she does sing	they do sing

WHAT USES DOES IT HAVE?

The **simple present** is used for:

1. an action (or state) occurring in the present:

   *They **speak** Chinese.*

2. a habitual action (which is still true):

   *I always **study** in the evening.*

3. existing facts and eternal truths:

   *Paris **is** the capital of France.*   *I **think** therefore I **am.*** (Descartes)

The **present progressive** is used to:

1. stress the *continuing* nature of the verb's action in either a statement or a question:

   *I **am** still **trying!***   *__Are__ you **going** to the library now?*

2. make a future action more immediate:

   *We **are reading** this book next week.*   *I **am going** to the show tomorrow.*

The **present emphatic** is used to:

1. add stress or contradict:

   *I **do** want to do well.*   *They **do** not do that!*

2. form questions or negative statements:

   *__Do__ you **go** to the lake in the summer?*
   *I **do** not **know** what you are talking about.*

3. "-re" verbs. Drop the *-re* and add *-s, -s,* (nothing); *-ons, -ez, -ent:*

Person	Singular	Plural
1	je rends	nous rendons
2	tu rends	vous rendez
3	il rend	elles rendent

WHAT USES DOES IT HAVE?

1. All of the uses listed for the three present tenses in English are filled by this one tense in French. There is an idiom, *être en train de + infinitive*, if you must emphasize being in the act of doing something:

   *Je ne veux pas sortir maintenant; je **suis en train de préparer** notre dîner.*
   I don't want to go out now; I'm in the middle of fixing our dinner.

2. French uses the present with *depuis* for an action begun in the past which is still going on in the present:

   *J'**attends** la lettre **depuis** dix jours.*
   I have been waiting for the letter for ten days. (I began waiting ten days ago, and I am still waiting.)

Past Tenses in English

WHAT ARE THEY? The past tenses are used to describe actions (or states) in the past.

WHAT FORMS DO THEY HAVE? There are three past tenses corresponding to the three present tenses discussed previously. (For perfect tenses, see pp. 98–107.)

The **simple past** is the second principal part of the verb (see p. 80). It is not inflected; all of the forms are the same. The simple past of weak verbs ends in "-ed", e.g., *talked, wished.* Strong verbs are all irregular:

Person	Singular	Plural
1	I sang	we sang
2	you sang	you sang
3	she sang	they sang

The **past progressive** is formed by the simple past of the verb "to be" plus the present participle of the main verb:

Person	Singular	Plural
1	I was singing	we were singing
2	you were singing	you were singing
3	she was singing	they were singing

The **past emphatic** is formed with the simple past of "to do" plus the infinitive:

Person	Singular	Plural
1	I did sing	we did sing
2	you did sing	you did sing
3	he did sing	they did sing

WHAT USES DO THEY HAVE? The three past tenses closely parallel the three present tenses, except that the action takes place in the past. The simple past is a statement of a fact; the progressive emphasizes the duration or continuation of the action at a given moment in the past; the emphatic stresses the statement.

OTHER PAST FORMS. There are also expressions that provide special meanings:

IMMEDIATE PAST action: *to have just* plus past participle:

> Mary **has just arrived** this minute.

HABITUAL PAST action: *used to* or *would* plus infinitive:

> I **used to go** to the movies every week. For a long time I **would see** them every day.

REPEATED PAST action: *kept (on)* plus present participle:

> He **kept (on) doing** it.

Past Tenses in French (Imperfect Tense *[L'Imparfait]*)

WHAT FORMS DOES IT HAVE? The imperfect tense is formed with a stem plus particular endings. The stem is formed by dropping the "-ons" from the first person plural of the present:

Parler	Finir	Dormir	Rendre
(nous parl-)	(nous finiss-)	(nous dorm-)	(nous rend-)
je parlais	je finissais	je dormais	je rendais
tu parlais	tu finissais	tu dormais	tu rendais
elle parlait	il finissait	elle dormait	il rendait
nous parlions	nous finissions	nous dormions	nous rendions
vous parliez	vous finissiez	vous dormiez	vous rendiez
ils parlaient	elles finissaient	ils dormaient	elles rendaient

NOTE: *Être* is the only verb that is irregular in the imperfect. The stem is *ét-*. The endings are regular (*j'étais, nous étions*, etc.). Some verbs that have only third person singular subjects are based on a "projected" form for *nous*, e.g., *falloir:* "nous fallons," imperfect: *il fallait*.

WHAT USES DOES IT HAVE? Use the imperfect for:

1. description: What you are describing is more important than the action.
2. habitual action: See the English "used to" construction.
3. duration or continuing action: See the English past progressive.
4. repeated action: See the English "kept on" construction.

NOTE: You must choose the tense on the basis of these principles, not on a one-to-one correspondence with English tenses or idioms. The imperfect is used many times when we would use the simple past in English:

*C'était lundi et il **pleuvait**.* → It was Monday and it was raining. (description)
*J'**allais** à l'école quand j'**étais** enfant.* → I went to school when I was a child. (habitual action/description)
*Il **lisait** toute la soireé.* → He read all evening. (duration)

OTHER PAST TENSES. Other tenses used to describe past time are **passé composé** (see p. 99); **pluperfect** (see p. 102); **passé simple** and **passé antérieur** (see p. 121–122); and **past subjunctive** (see pp. 114, 122).

IMPARFAIT VS. PASSÉ COMPOSÉ (completed action; duration not important):

Passé Composé	Imparfait
Event happened once	Event happened often (repeated/habitual)
Finished and completed event	Continuing, unfinished event
Series of distinct events	Description

*Elle **a fini** ses devoirs.*	*Elle **finissait** souvent très tard.*
*Le téléphone **a sonné** pendant qu'il **dormait**.*	
*Jean **est arrivé** à Paris, **a trouvé** un hôtel, et y **est resté**.*	*Jean **était** un étudiant américain qui **arrivait** à Paris en juin et y **passait** ses vacances.*

OTHER PAST FORMS

1. For the immediate past, use **venir de** plus an infinitive:

   *Marie **vient** d'arriver.* → Mary has just arrived.

2. For "used to" or "would" plus infinitive, use the imperfect tense.

Future Tenses in English

WHAT ARE THEY? The future tenses are used to describe events that have not yet taken place.

WHAT FORMS DO THEY HAVE? There are only two tenses for future time: the future and the future progressive. Both are compound tenses, i.e., they require more than one word to form them. The **future** is formed by using the auxiliary (helping) verb "will" plus the infinitive of the main verb:

Person	Singular	Plural
1	I will sing	we will sing
2	you will sing	you will sing
3	he will sing	they will sing

The **future progressive** is formed with the future of "to be" plus the present participle. It therefore requires three words:

Person	Singular	Plural
1	I will be singing	we will be singing
2	you will be singing	you will be singing
3	she will be singing	they will be singing

NOTE:

1. There are no irregular futures in English.
2. "Will" and "shall" are often abbreviated as " 'll": *We'll do it tomorrow. You'll be studying that next week.*
3. In very formal English, a distinction is made between the first person forms and those of the second and third persons. "Shall" is used for the "I" and "we" forms: *I **shall** sing. "We **shall** overcome."*
4. It was this distinction between the two auxiliary verbs that used to allow us an emphatic future form. Reversing the normal auxiliaries (*I **will** speak! They **shall** not pass!*) constituted the future emphatic. These forms, however, are now largely ignored.

WHAT USES DO THEY HAVE? The distinction between the future and the future progressive is the same as that between the corresponding tenses in the present (see p. 90). They are used:

1. to express an action or state that will happen or exist in the future.
2. in conditional sentences Type 1, when the "if" clause is in the present:

   *If you **study**, you **will succeed**.* (See the ✔ **Quick Check,** p. 107.)

OTHER FUTURE FORMS. Another way of indicating future tense is an idiomatic use of "to go." The present tense of "to go" plus the infinitive of the main verb indicates future time:

*I **am going to sing** tomorrow.*

Future Tense in French

WHAT FORMS DOES IT HAVE? There is only one future tense in French. It is formed with the stem plus particular endings:

Stem: the full infinitive (or up to the final "r" for "-re" verbs)
Endings: *-ai, -as, -a, -ons, -ez, -ont*

NOTE:

1. Future stems always end in "r."

2. The endings are the same as the present tense of *avoir* except that there is no "av-" in the first and second persons plural:

Parler	Finir	Dormir	Rendre (drop the "-e")	Être (irregular)
je parlerai	je finirai	je dormirai	je rendrai	je serai
tu parleras	tu finiras	tu dormiras	tu rendras	tu seras
il parlera	elle finira	il dormira	elle rendra	elle sera
nous parlerons	nous finirons	nous dormirons	nous rendrons	nous serons
vous parlerez	vous finirez	vous dormirez	vous rendrez	vous serez
elles parleront	ils finiront	elles dormiront	ils rendront	ils seront

There are a number of verbs with irregular stems in the future. All endings are regular:

avoir = aur-	venir = viendr-
savoir = saur-	tenir = tiendr-
être = ser-	recevoir = recevr-
aller = ir-	devoir = devr-
faire = fer-	pleuvoir = pleuvr-
voir = verr-	vouloir = voudr-
envoyer = enverr-	valoir = vaudr-
mourir = mourr-	falloir = faudr-
courir = courr-	
pouvoir = pourr-	

NOTE: "-er" verbs that have a spelling change before a mute "e" in the present (e.g., *payer → je paie; appeler → j'appelle; acheter → j'achète*) make this change in the future also since the last "e" is mute when it is part of the future stem: *je paierai; j'appellerai; j'achèterai*, etc.

WHAT USES DOES IT HAVE? The future is used:

1. to express an action or state that will happen or exist.

2. in conditional sentences Type 1, when the "if" clause is in the present:

    *Si vous **étudiez**, vous **réussirez**.* (See the ✔ **Quick Check**, p. 107.)

3. after *quand, lorsque, dès que*, and *aussitôt que* when you mean the future:

    *Quand il **arrivera**, nous dînerons.* (He's not here yet.)
    *Je vous l'expliquerai, dès que je le **comprendrai** moi-même.* (I don't understand yet.)

OTHER FUTURE FORMS. As we use "to go" in English, we may use the present tense of *aller* plus the infinitive of the main verb to express future time or intention in French:

*Je **vais chanter** demain.*

Conditional Tense in English

WHAT IS IT? Many grammarians—even those who accept more than the present and the past as tenses—no longer consider the conditional to be a true tense, but rather a mood. This may be because its structure can convey a number of other meanings. We will consider it as a tense here, however, since it will help you to see the parallels with French.

WHAT FORMS DOES IT HAVE? The conditional is formed with the auxiliary verb "would" plus the infinitive of the main verb:

Person	Singular	Plural
1	I would sing	we would sing
2	you would sing	you would sing
3	she would sing	they would sing

The **conditional progressive** tense is formed with the conditional of "to be" plus the present participle. It therefore requires three words:

Person	Singular	Plural
1	I would be singing	we would be singing
2	you would be singing	you would be singing
3	she would be singing	they would be singing

NOTE: The same distinction occurs with the conditional auxiliary as you saw with the future. In very formal English *should* is used in place of *would* for the first person forms, e.g., **I should sing, but you would** not. However, confusion with *should* meaning *ought to* is a real problem here, and these forms have fallen into disuse. You will still find them occasionally, especially in older writing.

Would and *should* are often abbreviated as " 'd": **I'd** *go if you did.*

WHAT USES DOES IT HAVE? The conditional is used for:

1. conditional sentences Type 2:

    If ___condition___ , (then) ___result___ .

    *If I were rich,   (then)   I **would go** to Europe every year.*

2. to convey the future from a past perspective:

    *On Sunday, John said: "OK, I **will** see you on Monday." (future)*
    *On Tuesday, Robert says: "John said that he **would** see us on Monday." (conditional)*

Conditional Tense in French

WHAT IS IT? In French, the conditional is often considered a mood, rather than a tense, since it expresses speculation, not facts. This distinction, however, has no practical effect on its forms or uses.

WHAT FORM DOES IT HAVE? The conditional tense is formed with:

Stem: the same as the future for every verb, regular and irregular (see p. 95).

Endings: the same as the *imparfait* in every case (see p. 93). There are no verbs that do not follow this pattern.

Parler (fut: je parlerai)	**Finir** (fut: je finirai)	**Dormir** (fut: je dormirai)	**Rendre** (fut: je rendrai)	**Être** (fut: je serai)
je parlerais	je finirais	je dormirais	je rendrais	je serais
tu parlerais	tu finirais	tu dormirais	tu rendrais	tu serais
il parlerait	elle finirait	il dormirait	elle rendrait	il serait
nous parlerions	nous finirions	nous dormirions	nous rendrions	nous serions
vous parleriez	vous finiriez	vous dormiriez	vous rendriez	vous seriez
elles parleraient	ils finiraient	elles dormiraient	ils rendraient	ils seraient

NOTE: Since the conditional stem is the same as the future stem, follow the same rules for spelling-change verbs (see NOTE, p. 95): *j'appellerais; je paierais; j'achèterais,* etc.

WHAT USES DOES IT HAVE? The conditional in French is used the same ways as in English:

1. conditional sentences Type 2 (see ✔ **Quick Check,** p. 107):

   Si <u>condition (*imparfait*)</u> , <u>   result (*conditional*)   </u> .

   Si j'étais riche,   j'irais en Europe tous les ans.

2. to convey the future from a past perspective:

   *Dimanche Jean a dit: "OK, je vous **verrai** lundi."*
   *Mardi Robert dit: "Jean a dit qu'il nous **verrait** lundi."*

Perfect Tenses in English

WHAT ARE THEY? Perfect tenses express two ideas:

1. the time of the action or state
2. the fact that it is completed

"Perfect" in this sense comes from the Latin *perfectus* meaning "finished" or "completed." If something has been perfected, it does not need any further work. "Perfect" here, then, does not mean "ideal."

WHAT KINDS ARE THERE? There are two perfect tenses corresponding to each of the times we have already discussed: present, past, future, and conditional.

Present Perfect Tense in English

WHAT FORMS DOES IT HAVE? The present perfect is formed with the present tense of "to have" plus the past participle of the main verb:

Person	Singular	Plural
1	I have sung	we have sung
2	you have sung	you have sung
3	he has sung	they have sung

WHAT USES DOES IT HAVE? This tense indicates that from the point of view of the present time, the action has been completed.

COMPARE: *I **saw** that movie yesterday.*
            *I **have seen** that movie.*

The first is emphasizing a *past* action, "saw," or what I did yesterday. The second is emphasizing that I am *presently* experienced with that movie: I *now know* what it is about, i.e., I *have* (present) *seen* (completed, finished with) that movie.

An idiomatic use of this tense is associated with the words *for* or *since:*

*I **have tried for** three hours to phone him.*
*I **have tried since** five o'clock to phone him.*

When we use the present perfect, we are implying that there is a momentary respite, but that the three hours of trying have lasted up to the present.

Perfect (Compound) Tenses in French

WHAT FORMS DO THEY HAVE? All active voice perfect tenses are formed with a single auxiliary and the past participle of the main verb. (See p. 86 for forming the participles.)

WHAT KINDS ARE THERE? In French there is a perfect tense corresponding to each of the simple (one-word) tenses. They are used much as their English counterparts except for the first, which we call the **passé composé,** since its use differs greatly from the English tense that is formed in the same way. There is also one, the *passé surcomposé,* that we will not study; it is used only for reading (see Appendix IV, p. 121).

Passé Composé

WHAT FORMS ARE THERE? The passé composé is formed with the present tense of the auxiliary plus the past participle of the main verb.

AUXILIARIES. There are two possible auxiliaries in French (as in German, Italian, etc.). English used to have a second form, "the hour **is** come," but it is now considered antiquated. **Avoir** is the more common auxiliary and is used with the large majority of verbs. **Être** is used:

1. with a small group of verbs (fewer than 20)—all intransitive, many expressing motion. Many verbs formed from these verbs by adding a prefix also use **être** (*venir → revenir, devenir, parvenir,* etc.).

   NOTE: Some of these verbs may be used transitively. For example, *monter* can mean "to go up" (intransitive) or "to carry up" (transitive):

   *Je **suis monté** au premier.* → I went up to the second floor. (intransitive) BUT:
   *J'**ai monté** l'escalier.* → I climbed the stairs. (transitive)
   *J'**ai monté** ma valise.* → I carried up my suitcase. (transitive)
   *Elle **est sortie.*** → She went out. (intransitive) BUT:
   *Elle **a sorti** le livre de la bibliothèque.* → She took the book out of the library. (transitive)

   Avoir must be used with sentences that have direct objects (i.e., the verb is transitive).

2. with *any* verb that is used reflexively or reciprocally:

   *Nous nous **sommes rencontrés** à 5 heures.* → We met at 5 o'clock.
   *Ils **se sont parlé.*** → They talked to each other.

To see a helpful way to remember the verbs that commonly use *être* as their auxiliary, turn to the diagram at the bottom of p. 100.

(Continued on p. 101)

Present Perfect Progressive Tense in English

All progressive tenses emphasize *duration,* and all are conjugated with the auxiliary verb "to be" plus the present participle of the main verb.

WHAT FORMS DOES IT HAVE? To form the present perfect progressive, it follows, then, that the verb "to be" is in the present perfect while the main verb is expressed by its present participle:

Person	Singular	Plural
1	I have been singing	we have been singing
2	you have been singing	you have been singing
3	she has been singing	they have been singing

WHAT USES DOES IT HAVE? As in other progressive tenses, this one emphasizes duration. Look at the example with *since* given previously for the present perfect. If, instead of *I have tried,* we had used *I have been trying for three hours to phone him,* we express not only a fact, but how long the three hours have seemed to us.

La Maison d'être: Common verbs that use *être* as their auxiliary

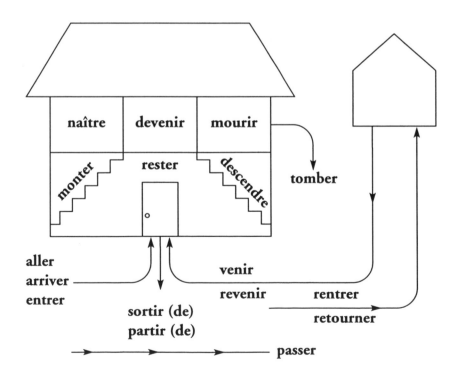

Perfect Tenses in French (continued)

Parler	Finir	Rendre	Aller
j'ai parlé	j'ai fini	j'ai rendu	je suis allé(e)
tu as parlé	tu as fini	tu as rendu	tu es allé(e)
il/elle/on a parlé	il/elle/on a fini	il/elle/on a rendu	il/elle/on est allé(e)
nous avons parlé	nous avons fini	nous avons rendu	nous sommes allé(e)s
vous avez parlé	vous avez fini	vous avez rendu	vous êtes allé(e)(s)
ils/elles ont parlé	ils/elles ont fini	ils/elles ont rendu	ils/elles sont allé(e)s

AGREEMENT OF THE PAST PARTICIPLE. Past participles are often used as adjectives. Then they agree with the noun they modify, as you would expect:

le français parlé (spoken French); *objets trouvés* (Lost and Found)

When used as part of a perfect tense, they follow one of two rules for agreement:

1. intransitive verbs conjugated with *être* agree with the subject:

   elle est **morte, nous** sommes **venus**

2. all other verbs agree with the direct object if it comes *before* the verb:

   *Voici **une maison**. Les Dupont **l**'ont **vendue** et c'est **celle** que Paul a **achetée**.*

NOTE: Be careful with reflexive pronoun objects. *Ils se sont vus* is clear, but some reflexives are *indirect* objects. Then there is NO agreement: *Ils se sont dit bonjour.*

✔ **QUICK CHECK**

NOTE: These rules apply to ALL perfect (compound) tenses, not just the passé composé.

Choosing the Right Auxiliary	Agreement of Past Participle
être: some intransitive verbs of motion	Rule 1: agrees with the subject
être: any verb used reflexively or reciprocally	Rule 2: agrees with the *direct* object when it comes before the verb
avoir: all other verbs	Rule 2: agrees with its noun when used as an adjective

WORD ORDER. For the most part, the auxiliary verb, the one that is conjugated, fills the same position as the simple-tense verb. Simply put the past participle at the end.

✔ **QUICK CHECK**

Il le dit.	*Il l'a dit.*
Il ne le dit pas.	*Il ne l'a pas dit.*
Le dit-il?	*L'a-t-il dit?*
Ne le dit-il pas?	*Ne l'a-t-il pas dit?*

WHAT USES DOES IT HAVE? The passé composé in French is used as we use the simple past in English, not necessarily as we use the present perfect, which *looks* like the passé composé. It refers to a *completed* action.

For other cases, you will need the imperfect. See p. 93 for contrasting uses of these two tenses.

Past Perfect (Pluperfect) Tense in English

WHAT IS IT? The past perfect tense tells us that some action (or state) was completed *before* some other past action (or state).

WHAT FORMS DOES IT HAVE? The past perfect tense is formed with the simple past of the auxiliary verb "to have" plus the past participle of the main verb:

Person	Singular	Plural
1	I had sung	we had sung
2	you had sung	you had sung
3	he/she/it had sung	they had sung

These forms are often contracted to "I'd," "you'd," etc.:

*I'd returned the book before you **asked** for it.*

WHAT USES DOES IT HAVE? Think of past time sequence in terms of "yesterday" (past) and "last week" (further in the past):

*Mary **had finished** her paper, before I **began.***
(past perfect; last week)   (past; yesterday)

Past Perfect Progressive Tense in English

WHAT IS IT? This tense shares the characteristics of the others that we have seen. It is:

past—viewpoint
perfect—completed
progressive—duration is stressed

WHAT FORMS DOES IT HAVE? The past perfect progressive tense is formed with the past perfect of the verb "to be" plus the present participle of the main verb:

Person	Singular	Plural
1	I had been singing	we had been singing
2	you had been singing	you had been singing
3	he had been singing	they had been singing

WHAT USES DOES IT HAVE? This tense expresses an action (or state) that had been continuing just before another past action:

*I **had been waiting** for three weeks when the letter **arrived.*** (The wait started over three weeks ago and continued up to yesterday, when the letter arrived.)

Past Perfect (Pluperfect) Tense in French

WHAT FORMS DOES IT HAVE? The past perfect tense is formed with the imperfect tense of the auxiliary *(avoir or être)* plus the past participle of the main verb:

Parler	Aller[*]
j'avais parlé	j'étais allé(e)
tu avais parlé	tu étais allé(e)
il/elle/on avait parlé	il/elle/on était allé(e)
nous avions parlé	nous étions allé(e)s
vous aviez parlé	vous étiez allé(e)(s)
ils/elles avaient parlé	ils/elles étaient allé(e)s

WHAT USES DOES IT HAVE? Just as in English, the past perfect tense refers to something completed further back in the past than some other past action or state:

Then . . . . **Now**

past perfect *(before)*   past   *(before)* present

*Marie **avait fini** son devoir, donc j'**ai commencé** à lui parler.*

[*] See p. 101 for agreement of the past participle.

Future Perfect Tense in English

WHAT IS IT? This tense expresses action that will be completed at some time in the future.

WHAT FORMS DOES IT HAVE? It is formed with the future of the auxiliary "to have" plus the past participle of the main verb:

Person	Singular	Plural
1	I will have sung	we will have sung
2	you will have sung	you will have sung
3	he/she will have sung	they will have sung

NOTE: These forms are often contracted in speech to "I'll've," etc.

WHAT USES DOES IT HAVE? It is used to express *future completion:*

*I **will have finished*** the book before the professor ***gives*** an exam.
(future perfect)   (present)

NOTE: In the second clause, we use the present tense in English, even though we are referring to the future. The professor is not giving an exam now.

Future Perfect Progressive Tense in English

WHAT IS IT? The future perfect progressive tense tells about an action (or state) that will be continued and then completed in the future.

WHAT FORMS DOES IT HAVE? It is formed with the future perfect tense of the auxiliary "to be" plus the present participle:

Person	Singular	Plural
1	I will have been singing	we will have been singing
2	you will have been singing	you will have been singing
3	she will have been singing	they will have been singing

WHAT USES DOES IT HAVE? It is used to emphasize the long duration of an action whose beginning is not specified but whose completion (at least provisionally) will be in the future:

*I **will have been studying*** English for 16 years when I ***graduate.***
(future perfect progressive)   (present)

Although graduation is in the future, English uses the present tense. We do not know from this sentence when I will graduate, nor do we know when I started to study English. The important point is the relationship between the verbs in the two clauses. In other words, 16 years of study *will be completed* at the moment in the future when I graduate.

Future Perfect Tense in French

WHAT FORMS DOES IT HAVE? The future perfect tense is formed with the auxiliary in the future tense plus the past participle:

Parler	**Aller**[*]
j'aurai parlé	je serai allé(e)
tu auras parlé	tu seras allé(e)
il/elle aura parlé	il/elle sera allé(e)
nous aurons parlé	nous serons allé(e)s
vous aurez parlé	vous serez allé(e)(s)
ils/elles auront parlé	ils/elles seront allé(e)s

WHAT USES DOES IT HAVE? The future perfect tense is used:

1. as in English.
2. after *quand, lorsque, dès que,* and *aussitôt que* if a future completed action is being described, even though we use the present in English (see p. 90):

   *Quand vous **viendrez,** j'**aurai terminé** mon travail.*
   When you come (sometime in the future), I will have finished my work.

   *Quand vous l'**aurez terminé,** nous le **discuterons.***
   When you have finished it *(sometime in the future),* we shall discuss it.

[*] See p. 101 for agreement of the past participle.

Conditional Perfect Tense in English

WHAT FORMS DOES IT HAVE? The conditional perfect tense is formed with the conditional tense of "to have" plus the past participle of the main verb:

Person	Singular	Plural
1	I would have sung	we would have sung
2	you would have sung	you would have sung
3	he/she would have sung	they would have sung

These forms are often contracted, especially in speech, to "I'd've, you'd've," etc.:

I'd've come if *I'd* known.

WHAT USES DOES IT HAVE? It is used primarily in the result clauses of Type 3 conditional sentences (see below):

He **would have** (would've) **seen** the film if he **had** (he'd) **known** that it was so good.
We **would have** (would've) **come** if we **had** (we'd) **known** about it.
   (conditional perfect)   (past perfect)

NOTE: The " 'd" in English is a contraction both of "had" and "would." This can cause some confusion unless you analyze what you mean:

If he**'d said** he needed it, I**'d've** given it to him.
(he had said [pluperfect]) (I would have given [cond. perf.])

✔ **QUICK CHECK.** The three most common types of conditional sentences:

"If" Clause	"Result" Clause	"If" Clause	"Result" Clause
1. If you **are** ready,	we **will** go.	present	future
2. If you **were** ready,	we **would** go.	subjunctive	conditional
3. If you **had been** ready,	we **would have** gone.	pluperfect	conditional perfect

Conditional Perfect Progressive Tense in English

WHAT FORMS DOES IT HAVE? The conditional perfect progressive tense is formed with the conditional perfect of the auxiliary "to be" plus the past participle of the main verb:

Person	Singular	Plural
1	I would have been singing	we would have been singing
2	you would have been singing	you would have been singing
3	she would have been singing	they would have been singing

Conditional Perfect Progressive Tense in English (continued)

WHAT USES DOES IT HAVE? This tense is used in the same way as the conditional perfect except that the idea of duration is added:

> *I **would** not **have been sleeping** when you arrived if I **had known** you were coming.*
> (conditional perfect progressive)   (past perfect)

Conditional Perfect Tense in French

WHAT FORMS DOES IT HAVE? The conditional perfect tense is formed by the conditional of the auxiliary plus the past participle of the main verb:

Parler	Aller
j'aurais parlé	je serais allé(e)
tu aurais parlé	tu serais allé(e)
il/elle/on aurait parlé	il/elle/on serait allé(e)
nous aurions parlé	nous serions allé(e)s
vous auriez parlé	vous seriez allé(e)(s)
ils/elles auraient parlé	ils/elles seraient allé(e)s

WHAT USES DOES IT HAVE? The conditional perfect tense is used, as in English, primarily for Type 3 conditional sentences:

> *Il **aurait vu** le film s'il **avait su** qu'il était si bon.*
> (conditional perfect)   (pluperfect)

> *Nous **serions venus** si nous en **avions su** quelque chose.*
> (conditional perfect)   (pluperfect)

✔ **QUICK CHECK.** The three types of conditional sentences:

"Si" Clause	"Result" Clause	"Si" Clause	"Result" Clause
1. Si vous **êtes** prêt,	nous **irons.**	present	future
2. Si vous **étiez** prêt,	nous **irions.**	imperfect	conditional
3. Si vous **aviez été** prêt,	nous y **serions allés.**	pluperfect	conditional perfect

Passive Voice in English

WHAT IS IT? The passive voice is the form used when the subject receives the verb action:

Active Voice:	Subject	Active Verb	Direct Object
	The **dog**	bit	**Susie.**
Passive Voice:	Subject	Passive Verb	Agent
	Susie	was bitten	by the **dog.**

Notice that the *direct object* of the active verb becomes the *subject* of the passive verb. The active verb's subject is placed after the passive verb in a prepositional phrase and is called the agent. It is not always expressed, as in the colloquial "John got caught." It is either not important or not known by whom or what he was caught.

WHAT FORMS DOES IT HAVE? The passive voice is formed with "to be" or "get" plus the past participle of the main verb.

NOTE: Only *transitive* verbs can be made passive.

Time	Active	Passive
Present	John catches the ball.	The ball **is caught** by John.
Past	The man read the book.	The book **was read** by the man.
Future	Mrs. Smith will lead the discussion.	The discussion **will be led** by Mrs. Smith.

The perfect and progressive tenses are formed in the same way. Some of the forms can get very long (e.g., the passive future progressive reads: "The work **will have been being done** at 3 P.M.") and are seldom used.

Passive Voice in French

WHAT FORMS DOES IT HAVE? The passive voice in French is always formed with the verb *être* plus the past participle of the main verb acting like an adjective, i.e., always agreeing with the subject. It may be in *any tense*.

Agency ("by") is usually expressed by *par* (but sometimes *de* is used):

Time	Active	Passive
Present	Jean attrape la balle.	La balle **est attrapée par** Jean.
Passé Composé	L'homme a lu le livre.	Le livre **a été lu par** l'homme.

All other tenses are formed by using the appropriate tense of *être* plus the past participle of the verb in question.

WHAT USES DOES IT HAVE? The French believe even more strongly than we do that the passive is a weak voice and that active voice is preferable. (Your English teacher may have suggested this as a means of improving your writing. Writers sometimes even tend to use less vivid language when speaking in the passive.) Compare the following sentences:

Passive	Active
Our receiver was tackled by their defensive end.	Their defensive end slammed our receiver to the ground.
This abstract was painted by Pablo Picasso.	Pablo Picasso created this colorful abstract.

If speakers of English are less than enthusiastic about the passive, the French actively dislike it. As a result it is seldom used. There are a number of ways to avoid it:

1. Turn the sentence around:

   Not: *Le livre a été lu par la classe.*   **But:** *La classe a lu le livre.*

2. Use *on:*

   Not: *Le français est parlé ici.*   **But:** *Ici on parle français.*

3. Use the reflexive:

   Not: *Hier les robes étaient vendues à bas prix.*   **But:** *Hier les robes se vendaient à bas prix.*

Imperative Mood in English

WHAT IS IT? The imperative mood is the command mood.

WHAT FORMS DOES IT HAVE? The forms of the imperative are very similar to those of the present indicative with a few exceptions. The imperative exists in only one form:

Second person (singular and plural the same): *Sing!*

For the first person plural and the third persons, the auxiliary verb "let" is used:

First person plural: *Let's (let us) sing!*
Third persons: *Let him (them) sing!*

NOTE: No subject is expressed for the imperative.

Irregular imperatives. There is only one irregular imperative in English: the verb "to be." Compare:

Indicative	**Imperative**
You are good.	*Be good!*
We are quiet.	*Let's be quiet!*

Imperative Mood in French

WHAT FORMS DOES IT HAVE? The imperative mood has three forms: second person familiar, second person formal, and the first person plural (the "let's" form in English). These forms are the same as the indicative except:

1. the subject is not expressed.

2. the "s" drops from the ending of "-er" verbs in the singular:

Parler	Finir	Dormir	Rendre
parle!	finis!	dors!	rends!
parlez!	finissez!	dormez!	rendez!
parlons!	finissons!	dormons!	rendons!

NOTE: The second person singular "-s" of "-er" verbs remains before the object pronouns *y* and *en:*

*Vas-y. **Parles**-en un peu.*

For the third person command, use the subjunctive mood (see pp. 113–115). "I want" is understood:

*Qu'elle **entre**!* → Let her enter! (I want her to enter!)
*Qu'ils **soient** tranquilles!* → Let them be quiet! (I want them to be quiet!)

Irregular imperatives. Only four verbs have irregular forms in the imperative mood:

avoir	aie	ayez	ayons
être	sois	soyez	soyons
savoir	sache	sachez	sachons
vouloir	—	veuillez	—

Veuillez is the form used when requesting something:

Veuillez être à l'heure demain. → Please be on time tomorrow.

WORD ORDER. In *affirmative* commands, pronoun objects follow the verb and are attached to it by a hyphen. The direct object always precedes the indirect (see p. 30):

Donnez-le-moi!   *Dites-le-lui!*

In *negative* commands, the objects return to their normal position and order:

Ne me le donnez pas!   *Ne le lui dites pas!*

Subjunctive Mood in English

WHAT IS IT? The subjunctive is the mood that expresses what *may* be true.

WHAT FORMS DOES IT HAVE? The subjunctive does not change for persons. The **present subjunctive** (or the auxiliary verb in a compound tense) is always the same: the basic, or infinitive, form of the verb. Therefore, it is different from the indicative only:

1. For the third person singular:

   that he take, that she have

2. For the verb "to be":

Present	**Past**
that I be, that he be, etc.	*that I were, that she were,* etc.

WHAT USES DOES IT HAVE? The subjunctive is used only infrequently in English. For that reason, we tend to disregard it except in certain fixed expressions. Nevertheless, it does have some specific uses that are important in formal English:

1. Contrary-to-fact conditions:

   *If I **were** you... "If this **be** madness, yet there is method in it."* (Hamlet)

2. After verbs such as *wish, suppose, insist, urge, demand, ask, recommend, suggest*:

   I wish that he **were** able to come.   They insisted that we **be** present.
   *I recommend that he **learn** the subjunctive.*

3. After some impersonal expressions, such as *it is necessary, it is important*:

   *It is important that he **avoid** errors.   It is necessary that Mary **see** its use.*

4. In some fixed expressions:

   *So **be** it! Long **live** the Queen! Heaven **forbid**! Far **be** it from me to suggest that!*

NOTE: Most of the fixed expressions are a way of expressing a third person imperative. The idea "I wish that" is implied, but not expressed.

   Whenever possible (except for the fixed expressions), we tend to use an alternative expression, usually with modals (auxiliaries) in order to avoid the subjunctive in conversation and informal writing. Compare these sentences with the examples above:

1. *I wish that he **could come.***
2. *I told her that she **must learn** the subjunctive.*
3. *It is important for him **to avoid** errors.*
4. *Mary **needs to see** its importance.*

Subjunctive Mood in French

WHAT FORMS DOES IT HAVE? The subjunctive is fully conjugated in French. (We will study only the present and past tenses in the subjunctive mood, since that is enough for the large majority of cases.) The **present subjunctive** is formed with:

Stem: drop the "-ent" of the third person plural of the indicative
Endings: *-e, -es, -e; -ions, -iez, -ent*

The subjunctive forms for "-er" verbs are often exactly like the indicative except for the first and second person plural:

Parler (ils/elles parl*ent*)	Finir (ils/elles finiss*ent*)	Dormir (ils/elles dorm*ent*)	Rendre (ils/elles rend*ent*)
que je parle	que je finisse	que je dorme	que je rende
que tu parles	que tu finisses	que tu dormes	que tu rendes
qu'il/elle/on parle	qu'il/elle/on finisse	qu'il/elle/on dorme	qu'il/elle/on rende
que nous parlions	que nous finissions	que nous dormions	que nous rendions
que vous parliez	que vous finissiez	que vous dormiez	que vous rendiez
qu'ils/elles parlent	qu'ils/elles finissent	qu'ils/elles dorment	qu'ils/elles rendent

Que is before the subjunctive forms because they are used only in subordinate clauses (even if the main clause is not expressed).

Irregular subjunctives. Only two verbs have irregular endings. They are *avoir* and *être:*

Avoir		Être	
que j'aie	que nous ayons	que je sois	que nous soyons
que tu aies	que vous ayez	que tu sois	que vous soyez
qu'il/elle ait	qu'ils/elles aient	qu'il/elle soit	qu'ils/elles soient

Other verbs that have an irregular stem, but add the regular subjunctive endings are:

pouvoir → *que je* **puisse**
avoir → *que je* **sache**
faire → *que je* **fasse**
falloir → *qu'il* **faille** (exists only in third person singular)

In addition, a number of verbs that change the stem for the "nous" and "vous" forms in the present indicative also make this change in the present subjunctive:

Infinitive	Stem	Second Stem
aller	que j'aille	que nous allions
vouloir	que je veuille	que nous voulions
boire	que je boive	que nous buvions
venir	que je vienne	que nous venions

(Continued on p. 114)

Subjunctive
Mood in French
(continued)

You can easily recognize the **past subjunctive,** since its forms are the same as those for the passé composé except that the auxiliary is in the present subjunctive:

*qui j'**aie parlé**; qu'elle **soit venue***

WHAT USES DOES IT HAVE? In *theory,* the subjunctive is used to show that what you are saying is:

1. potentially (but not actually) true.
2. colored by emotion (which often distorts facts).
3. expressing your attitude toward something (rather than the actual facts).
4. doubtful, probably nonexistent, or not true.

In *practice,* there are certain words and expressions that require the subjunctive. The theory may help you to remember which ones they are, but you cannot argue theory against practice. If an expression requires the subjunctive, then it must be used whether or not you believe that it fits well into the theoretical bases.

The subjunctive is used principally:

1. after verbs or other expressions conveying the subject's emotional reactions:

   *je suis **content** que...*   *il **craint** que...*   *elles **regrettent** que...*

2. after verbs such as *vouloir, supposer, exiger,* and *demander* when there is a change of subject:

   Je veux qu'il vienne.   **Je** veux venir.*

   Note that the infinitive is used when there is no change of subject.

3. after some impersonal expressions when uncertainty is conveyed. Contrast the following lists:

Subjunctive	Indicative
il est peu probable que	il est probable que
il est possible que	il est vrai que
il est incroyable que	il est certain que
il semble que	il me semble que
il est étonnant que	il paraît que
il est souhaitable que	
il est bon que	
il vaut mieux que	

4. after conjunctions expressing:

   concession: *quoique; bien que*

   purpose: *pour que; afin que*

   indefinite time: *jusqu'à ce que; avant que*

   negation: *sans que; à moins que*

5. after superlatives (because of possible emotional exaggeration). Contrast:

   *C'est le plus beau poème que je **connaisse**.* (a personal opinion, therefore subjunctive)
   *New York est la plus grande ville que j'ai jamais **visitée**.* (a fact, therefore indicative)

   One is an emotion; one is a fact. The indicative and subjunctive respectively tell your audience how you mean the statement. Some French people do not make this distinction and use the subjunctive in all cases.

6. after some verbs (especially *penser* and *croire*) in the negative and interrogative, because asking what someone thinks, or saying what someone does not believe, implies doubt about the true situation. The negative-interrogative *Ne pensez-vous pas que...?* often takes the indicative because you expect a positive response.

7. for third person commands (see p. 111).

8. in certain fixed expressions: *Vive le roi!; À Dieu ne plaise!;* etc.

To remember the principal uses of the subjunctive in French, think of **SWAP NEEDS:**

S	seeming
W	wishing
A	asking
P	possibility
N	necessity
E	emotion
E	exaggeration
D	demanding
S	supposing

HOW TO AVOID THE SUBJUNCTIVE IN FRENCH

The subjunctive is used *only* in subordinate clauses (even if the main clause is not expressed, but only understood) and then only when the subjects of the two clauses are different. If the subject remains the same, you may avoid the subjunctive by:

1. using the infinitive. Contrast:

   Je suis content que vous soyez ici. (different subject)
   Je suis content d'être ici. (same person throughout)

2. using the indirect object pronoun with impersonal expressions. Contrast:

   Il faut que je parte.
   Il me faut partir. (not as common in everyday use)

APPENDIX I
Pronoun Review

PERSONAL PRONOUNS

	Always Used with a Verb			May Be Used Alone
SUBJECTS	**OBJECTS**			
	Direct	**Reflexive**	**Indirect**	**Disjunctive**
je	me	me	me	moi
tu	te	te	te	toi
il, elle, on	le, la	se	lui	lui, elle, soi
nous	nous	nous	nous	nous
vous	vous	vous	vous	vous
ils, elles	les	se	leur	eux, elles

COMPARISON OF RELATIVE AND INTERROGATIVE PRONOUNS

Relatives

	Person	Thing	Indefinite
Subject	qui (*or form of* lequel)	qui (*or form of* lequel)	ce qui
Object	que	que (*or form of* lequel)	ce que
Object of *de*	de qui (*or* dont)	dont (*or form of* duquel)	ce dont
Object of Any Other Preposition	prep. + qui (*or form of* lequel)	prep. + *form of* lequel où (for *time* or *place*)	ce + prep. + quoi

Interrogatives (Short Form)

	Person	Thing
Subject	qui	—
Object	qui	que
Object of Preposition	prep. + qui	prep. + quoi

Interrogatives (Long Form)

Interrogative pronoun + *est-ce* + relative pronoun

	Person	**Thing**
Subject	qui est-ce qui	qu'est-ce qui
Object	qui est-ce que	qu'est-ce que

ADJECTIVES VS. PRONOUNS

Demonstrative Adjectives and Pronouns

	Adjectives (*used with a noun*)	**Pronouns** (*used without a noun*)
Masculine Singular	ce livre (-ci, là)	celui (-ci, -là *or a prepositional phrase*)
Masculine Singular before Vowels or a Mute "h"	cet homme	celui
Feminine Singular	cette dame	celle
Masculine Plural	ces étudiants	ceux
Feminine Plural	ces étudiantes	celles

INTERROGATIVE ADJECTIVES AND PRONOUNS

	Adjectives (*used with a noun*)	**Pronouns** (*used without a noun*)
Masculine Singular	quel livre?	lequel?
Feminine Singular	quelle dame?	laquelle?
Masculine Plural	quels étudiants?	lesquels?
Feminine Plural	quelles filles?	lesquelles?

NOTE: The four forms of *lequel* are also used as relative pronouns (see p. 117).

APPENDIX II
Determiners: Summary

Normally use only one determiner before each noun.

Determiners for words beginning with a consonant or aspirate "h":

Masculine Singular	Feminine Singular	Plural
un café, mon héros	une glace, une haine	des livres, des tables, des héros
le café	la glace	les livres, les tables
		trois livres, trois tables, etc.
mon café, ton café, etc.	ma glace, ta glace, etc.	mes livres, tes livres, etc.
ce café	cette glace	ces livres, ces tables
quel café	quelle glace	quels livres, quelles tables
quelque café	quelque glace	quelques livres, quelques tables
du café, du homard	de la glace	des livres, des tables, des homards

Determiners for words beginning with a vowel or mute "h":

Masculine Singular	Feminine Singular	Plural
un amour	une eau	All of these forms are
l'amour, l'hôtel	l'eau	the same as the plural
mon amour, ton amour, etc.	mon eau, ton eau, etc.	forms above.
cet amour	cette eau	
quel amour	quelle eau	
de l'amour	de l'eau	

There are some occasions when no determiner is needed:

1. after some prepositions, e.g., *sans* (*sans doute*).
2. when a noun of nationality, profession, or religion is used to describe, e.g., *il est américain*.
3. when one noun is used to describe another, e.g., *un professeur d'art, une fête de famille*.
4. possession, e.g., *l'ami d'Henri*.
5. in a partitive under special circumstances (see p. 21).

APPENDIX III
Some Common Irregular Verbs

Pattern I. **L-shaped** verbs. Spelling change, including accents, in the singular and third person plural forms:

mener, acheter, geler, jeter, appeler, payer, envoyer, ennuyer, mourir, mouvoir, pouvoir, vouloir, venir, revenir, devenir, prévenir, tenir, retenir

Pattern II. **Box** verbs where singular forms are regular:

faire, taire, plaire, traire, voir,** croire, boire, haïr,** vêtir, fuir, cuire, nuire, écrire, suffire, rire, courir, prendre, comprendre, apprendre, surprendre, pendre, coudre, moudre*

Pattern III. **Box** verbs where plural forms are regular:

battre, mettre, permettre, promettre, soumettre, servir, partir, mentir, sortir, dormir, sentir, savoir, vêtir, valoir, suivre, vivre

Pattern IV. **Mistaken identity** verbs. "-ir" verbs that take "-er" endings:

offrir, souffrir, ouvrir, couvrir, découvrir, cueillir, accueillir, recueillir

Pattern V. **Disappearing letter** verbs. Infinitives whose final consonant sound is silent when the infinitive ending is dropped; since the final consonant has no sound, it is not written in the singular forms:

naître, connaître,* paître;* croître,* accroître;**

craindre, plaindre, atteindre, éteindre, peindre; joindre; résoudre; partir, sortir, mentir, dormir, sentir, servir; suivre, vivre; mettre, battre, pleuvoir

Pattern VI. **Soft consonant** verbs. "-ger" verbs add an "e" after the "g" and "-cer" verbs place a cedilla under the "c" ("ç") whenever the verb ending begins with any letter other than "e" or "i":

manger, commencer, placer

Pattern VII. **Change under stress** verbs. "-evoir" verbs are regular in the *nous/vous* forms, but change the "e" of the stem to "oi," when the stress is on the stem (see Pattern I) and eliminate the "v" in the singular forms (see Pattern V):

devoir, recevoir, percevoir, s'apercevoir

Verbs whose infinitives end in "-aître," "-oître," "-indre," "-yer" (except "-eyer"), and "-evoir" follow the same patterns within their groups:

connaître, craindre, essayer, devoir

Some irregular verbs that have patterns all their own include:

avoir, être, aller, falloir, vaincre (regular in sound; "c" and "qu" have the same sound), *bouillir, s'asseoir*

avoir	être	aller	falloir
j'ai	je suis	je vais	
tu as	tu es	tu vas	
il a	elle est	il va	il faut
nous avons	nous sommes	nous allons	
vous avez	vous êtes	vous allez	
elles ont	ils sont	elles vont	

* -ît (third person singular ending)

** -r (infinitive ending)

APPENDIX IV
Verbs for Reading

There are a few verb tenses not mentioned earlier which are found in reading. You do not need to learn these tenses now; you need only to be able to recognize them. They are literary tenses, never used in conversation or informal writing, but only in formal writing (e.g., literature, newspapers, scholarship, and formal speeches).

Passé Simple and Passé Antérieur

These are the literary equivalents of the *passé composé* and the *pluperfect*, respectively. They are translated in the same way, but using them gives a special formal tone to the writing and shows seriousness of purpose. Remember that for now it is enough to simply recognize them when you see them.

You will notice that there are three groups of endings for the *passé simple* and that ALL verbs use one of these three groups. This means that for irregular verbs, once you know the first form, all the other forms can be derived from it. Simply use the endings as you see them in the regular verbs. Notice that irregular *passé simple* stems often resemble either the past participle (e.g., *connaître* → *connu* → *je connus*) or the alternative stem in the present—the one used for the "nous" and "vous" forms if they are different (e.g., *écrire* → *nous écrivons* → *j'écrivis*).

For the few very irregular stems, the ancient Romans must often take responsibility. For instance, for the verb "être," the *passé simple* "je fus" comes from the Latin simple past of "to be": "fui." Once you have learned the *passé simple* of "être" and "avoir," you know the *passé antérieur*, which uses the *passé simple* of the auxiliary verb plus the past participle of the main verb. Otherwise, it follows all of the rules that you learned for the *passé composé*.

Imperfect Subjunctive and Pluperfect Subjunctive

These are also literary tenses and are used only in the kinds of writing discussed above. They are easy to recognize because of all the s's in most of the endings.

The imperfect subjunctive is formed from the same stem as the *passé simple*, so once you can recognize the irregular stems for the *passé simple*, you will also know the imperfect subjunctive. The pluperfect subjunctive uses the imperfect subjunctive of the auxiliary verb plus the past participle of the main verb. All other rules are the same as those for all the perfect tenses.

Therefore, all that really needs to be recognized are the stems and endings for the *passé simple* and you will know what you need to know for all four of these tenses.

PASSÉ SIMPLE

Parler ("-er" verbs)	**Finir** ("-ir" and "-re" verbs)	**Connaître** ("-re" and "-oir" verbs)	**Avoir**
je parlai	je finis	je connus	j'eus
tu parlas	tu finis	tu connus	tu eus
il/elle/on parla	il/elle/on finit	il connut	il eut
nous parlâmes	nous finîmes	nous connûmes	nous eûmes
vous parlâtes	vous finîtes	vous connûtes	vous eûtes
ils/elles parlèrent	ils/elles finirent	ils/elles connurent	ils/elles eurent

Verbs with irregular stems in the *passé simple* include the following. Note that the past participle often serves as the stem of the *passé simple:*

s'asseoir: je m'assis	être: je fus	recevoir: je reçus
craindre: je craignis	courir: je courus	savoir: je sus
écrire: j'écrivis	croire: je crus	se taire: je me tus
joindre: je joignis	devoir: je dus	valoir: je valus
faire: je fis	falloir: il fallut	vivre: je vécus
mettre: je mis	lire: je lus	vouloir: je voulus
naître: je naquis	plaire: je plus	venir: je vins
prendre: je pris	pleuvoir: il plut	tenir: je tins
voir: je vis	pouvoir: je pus	

PASSÉ ANTÉRIEUR

Formed with the auxiliary verb (*avoir* or *être*) in the *passé simple* plus the past participle:

Parler	Finir	Connaître	Être
j'eus parlé	j'eus fini	j'eus connu	j'eus été
tu eus parlé	tu eus fini	tu eus connu	tu eus été
etc.	etc.	etc.	etc.

Verbs taking *être* in the *passé composé* do so here, e.g., *elle fut allée, nous vous fûmes levés.*

IMPERFECT SUBJUNCTIVE

Parler	Finir	Connaître	Être
que je parlasse	que je finisse	que je connusse	que je fusse
que tu parlasses	que tu finisses	que tu connusses	que tu fusses
qu'il/elle parlât	qu'il/elle finît	qu'il/elle connût	qu'il fût
que nous parlassions	que nous finissions	que nous connussions	que nous fussions
que vous parlassiez	que vous finissiez	que vous connussiez	que vous fussiez
qu'ils parlassent	qu'ils finissent	qu'ils connussent	qu'ils fussent

PLUPERFECT SUBJUNCTIVE

Parler	Finir	Connaître	Être
que j'eusse parlé	que j'eusse fini	que j'eusse connu	que j'eusse été
que tu eusses	parlé que tu eusses fini	que tu eusses connu	que tu eusses été
etc.	etc.	etc.	etc.

Verbs taking *être: qu'elle fût allée, que nous nous fussions levés.*

APPENDIX V
Compound Tenses

subject	(ne)	(object)	auxiliary	(pas)	(adverb)	past participle	
ÊTRE SPECIAL GROUP:*			*être*			*Agrees with subject*	
je	ne	y	suis	pas	souvent	arrivé(e)(s)	resté(e)(s)
tu	n'	en	es		vite	tombé(e)(s)	descendu(e)(s)
il (elle)			est		*etc.*	allé(e)(s)	mort(e)(s)
nous			sommes			entré(e)(s)	venu(e)(s)
vous			êtes			parti(e)(s)	né(e)(s)
ils			sont			sorti(e)(s)	
(elles)							

subject	(ne)	(object)	auxiliary	(pas)	(adverb)	past participle
REFLEXIVE/RECIPROCAL VERBS:			*être*			*Agrees with preceding direct object.*
je	ne	me	suis	pas	bien	amusé(e)(s)
tu		t'	es		encore	levé(e)(s)
il (elle)		s'	est		*etc.*	reposé(e)(s)
nous		nous	sommes			habillé(e)(s)
vous		vous	êtes			réveillé(e)(s)
ils		se	sont			lavé les mains**

subject	(ne)	(object)	auxiliary	(pas)	(adverb)	past participle	
ALL OTHER VERBS			*avoir*			*Agrees with preceding direct object.*	
						Regular	*Irregular*
je	ne	les	ai	pas	beaucoup	parlé	vouloir → voulu(e)(s)
tu		m'en	as		déjà	montré(e)(s)	avoir → eu(e)(s)
il (elle)		nous les	a		encore	donné(e)(s)	voir → vu(e)(s)
nous		vous en	avons		assez	répondu	pouvoir → pu
vous		les lui	avez		toujours	répondu	savoir → su
ils	n'	y	ont		bien	sorti(e)(s)	boire → bu(e)(s)
(elles)					*etc.*		lire → lu(e)(s)
							croire → cru(e)(s)
							faire → fait(e)(s)
							dire → dit(e)(s)
							écrire → écrit(e)(s)
							mettre → mis(e)(s)
							prendre → pris(e)(s)
							être → été
							etc.

*See p. 100 for a complete list of the verbs that commonly take *être* as their auxiliary.
**In this case, *les mains* is the direct object of the verb, and since it does not precede the verb, there is no agreement.

APPENDIX VI

Il est... versus C'est...

The following chart shows most the major uses of *c'est* versus *il est:*

Il est	C'est
1. Noun with no modifiers (often profession, nationality, or religion): *Il est français. Elles sont professeurs.*	1. Noun with modifiers: *C'est un grand homme. Ce sont de bons professeurs.*
2. Adjective: *Il est grand.*	2. Adjective when there is an indefinite referent: *C'est facile.* (an idea, a concept, not a specific noun)
3. When *il* refers to a particular noun: *Il (le livre) est facile.*	3. Pronoun: *C'est lui.*
4. Location: *Il est à Paris. Il est dans mon sac.*	4. Prepositional phrases other than location: *C'est à moi. C'est pour vous.*
5. Idioms, always used the same way: *Il est une heure.* (time)	5. Idioms, always used the same way: *C'est lundi. C'est demain le 23. Est-ce que...* (for questions)

NOTE: When introducing a clause, use *il est...* when the real subject will be stated later in the sentence. Use *c'est...* when the subject will not be stated.

Il est facile de faire cela. → It's easy to do that.
C'est facile à faire. → It's easy to do.

✔ **QUICK CHECK.** As a test, try to turn the sentence around. If you can, *il est...* is correct:

"To do that is easy." The sentence makes sense, therefore *il est...* is used in French.
"To do is easy." This sentence does not make sense as there is no subject. *C'est...* is used.